# The Bride's Diplomacy Guide

# Additional Wedding Guides by Sharon Naylor

*1000 Best Secrets for Your Perfect Wedding*
*1000 Best Wedding Bargains*
*1001 Ways to Have a Dazzling Second Wedding*
The Bridesmaid Handbook
The Busy Bride's Essential Wedding Checklists
The Complete Outdoor Wedding Planner
The Essential Guide to Wedding Etiquette
The Groom's Guide
How to Have a Fabulous Wedding for $10,000 or Less
How to Plan an Elegant Wedding in 6 Months or Less
The Mother-of-the-Bride Book
The Mother of the Groom
Renewing Your Wedding Vows: A Complete Planning Guide to Saying "I Still Do"
*Your Special Wedding Toasts*
*Your Special Wedding Vows*
The Ultimate Bridal Shower Idea Book
The Ultimate Wedding Registry Workbook
*What's Your Bridal Style?*
*Your Day, Your Way: The Essential Handbook for the 21st-Century Bride*
  (coauthor)

For a complete list, visit *www.sharonnaylor.net*.

# The Bride's Diplomacy Guide

## Guide

Solutions to **150** of the Stickiest
Dilemmas that Face a Bride-to-Be

*Sharon Naylor*

Aadamsmedia
Avon, Massachusetts

For Madison and Kevin

Published by
Adams Media, an F+W Publications Company
57 Littlefield Street, Avon, MA 02322. U.S.A.
*www.adamsmedia.com*

ISBN 10: 1-59869-322-0
ISBN 13: 978-1-59869-322-5

Printed in Canada

J I H G F E D C B A

Library of Congress Cataloging-in-Publication Data
is available from the publisher.

*This book is available at quantity discounts for bulk purchases.*
*For information, please call 1-800-289-0963.*

# Contents

# Introduction

Weddings make people crazy.

Your mild-mannered mom turns into a power freak, pressuring you into adding just twelve more of her friends to your already overcrowded guest list. Your future mother-in-law suddenly decides to latch on to her son and question your every move. Your parents think it's 1954 when it comes to what weddings cost and groan over every penny spent—even if you're paying for everything. Your bridesmaids start arguing—or not returning your calls—and the groomsmen joke about bringing strippers as their dates to your wedding. And your fiancé . . . let's just say he's either way too invested in the invitations, or he doesn't seem to care at all.

It's enough to make you a little bit crazy. But the solution to the myriad surprising and annoying things that people do and say is diplomacy. Great diplomacy. You can handle anything that people plant in front of you—the minefield of complaints, conflicts, requests, and overrulings (yes, overrulings of your plans!)—if you know how to cope with everyone in your life delicately and wisely.

What happens when you don't have good diplomacy skills? All those little irritating things that your mother, sister, bridesmaids, fiancé, wedding coordinator, and baker do will get stuffed inside of you and fester into resentment, and pretty soon you'll be on the TV show *Bridezillas* wearing your wedding gown, pointing your manicured finger, and yelling at your grandmother because she's wearing the wrong color pantyhose and her hair is too high. You'll be pouting, complaining to anyone who will listen until they stop taking your calls, gaining weight, melting down, snapping at your fiancé, and generally being less than the radiant bride you could be.

Even worse than bad behavior, your future relationships will be hurt. Not could be hurt, will be hurt—because you'll hurt others and also be hurt, and those injuries at this important time in your life can become a permanent part of your wedding memories. Many brides report that they don't speak to a former bridesmaid anymore due to arguments that stemmed from some conflict that good diplomacy could have defused. So many say they'll never be close to their mother-in-law because they're still simmering over the way she acted during the planning phase.

Granted, some people just have no consideration. Some people are bullies. Some are selfish. But most of the people in your life have just succumbed to a very common phenomenon: getting caught up in the emotion of a wedding. Moms tell me they regret how power hungry they became, that they shudder at how they spoke to their daughters, and that they'd go back and do it differently if they could. Bridesmaids say the same thing, shaking their heads at their own foolish behavior and self-centeredness. And everyone says they wish they knew better how to prevent the conflicts and attitudes that hurt their standing with the bride and groom. Brides and grooms are no different. They, too, get caught up in the emotions, the financial pressure, the time crunch, and all those outside opinions until they just snap.

Good diplomacy can prevent all of this.

You already have the makings of a good diplomat within you. It's more about character traits than about what you actually say. Here are the top character traits of a great diplomat:

- **Patience.** Knowing that not every problem can be solved in two minutes, and that some will need to be solved through a process, such as a series of conversations.
- **Empathy.** Sometimes, your friend or loved one is causing a problem because they have an altogether separate problem, and they're just taking their frustrations out on you and your wedding tasks. Try to look beneath their behavior with understanding.
- **Calmness.** If you're angry about the latest affront, take a few moments to calm down before you respond. Approach every person with a calm and gentle demeanor.
- **Self-Confidence.** Believe that you do have the ability to handle any issue. It isn't better to roll over and let others have their way. Healthy assertiveness is a big part of successful diplomacy.
- **Sense of Humor.** Some issues can be defused by laughing them off and not taking them too seriously.
- **Humility.** Don't take yourself—or your wedding—too seriously, either.
- **Perspective.** Always remember that your relationships will last long after the wedding. That's what's most important. And the wedding details are just to make the day more beautiful and more meaningful. The reason for your wedding

day is joining your life with your fiancé. When you look at that, the other issues will shrink in comparison.

Since you have this book in your hands, you've already taken the most important step toward eliminating conflict. You know that you can say and do the right things in any situation so that resentment doesn't begin to build. You won't be mad at yourself for not saying something when someone crosses the line. You'll have a guide to coach you through some of the trickiest wedding diplomacy scenarios, and you'll get effective wording suggestions here. Even if you're already in the middle of a conflict, if you're facing dicey dilemmas from your bridesmaids, parents, fiancé, vendors, or guests, you'll unravel them all now.

The 150 questions in this book came directly from brides and grooms just like you. These are the pressing concerns that couples have sent me through my Web site, www.sharonnaylor .net, and through my forums at www.PashWeddings.com and www .NJWedding.com. (So if there's a question you have that isn't covered in this book, you can write to me directly for an answer. Your entry might appear in future editions!) I've chosen the most common concerns of couples and their families from literally thousands of diplomacy questions that I've received over the past fifteen years. The answers are here for you to use, just as thousands of couples before you have successfully done. You'll find suggested scripts of non-threatening, diplomatic conversations for most of the scenarios throughout the book, including the best ways to approach a sticky subject and work through it with a parent, bridesmaid, or anyone else with whom you must carefully weigh your words. And since you know that in some cases they'll likely respond in a challenging way, you'll also get the best follow-up statements to use to guide the topic out of conflict and into resolution.

You've just taken on the role of diplomatic specialist for your wedding, and your skills are going to save your day, as well as your future relationships with everyone around you. You'll spot those landmines and step gracefully over them in your best shoes, and you'll share this wisdom with others around you, especially your fiancé, so that he can be your full partner in addressing those who have lost their minds—and that might be you on some days. Within the 150 tricky wedding diplomacy scenarios listed here are answers for *all* of you, so that you can solve each problem with grace, style, and self-confidence, and preserve an intact relationship with each "offender" afterward.

Will everything be solvable? Some people are intent on being difficult, so leave their larger issues to them (and their therapists), and apply your diplomacy to yourself. By that, I mean not letting some small-minded person destroy your happiness. Sometimes, the best diplomatic move is to turn away from that person's drama and focus on all those who haven't lost their minds, who are loving enough to remember that it's your wedding day and your happiness that matters most.

Let's get started.

# Chapter 1

# Problematic Parents: From Momzilla to Dad's New Girlfriend

Parents get very invested in your wedding plans. Not only financially, as they may or may not be contributing funds to your dream wedding, but also emotionally. They're also invested socially, since parents are often the ones spouting that ever-so-stressful question—"What will people think?"—when it comes to any original, nontraditional, or personal idea you have for your wedding. They may have their own dramas, such as divorces or longstanding feuds; or they may be terrified by the idea that you're getting married, which means they're getting older, losing you, facing an empty nest, or any number of other issues that could make them lose their minds during the happiest time of your life.

Diplomacy with parents can be a tricky thing, since you might not have much experience dealing with your parents on adult terms. Although you're an adult and you function with

1

self-assurance in all other areas of your life, you might still fall back into your role as Daddy's Little Girl or Mom's Adversary (or vice versa) at family gatherings. And, no matter how strong we are in our character and self-esteem, they can exert a lot of power over us. They know how to push our buttons, deliberately or unintentionally. Now this change in your life is blinking a great big flashing sign in front of all of you—"Things Are About to Change." These changes can cause parents to behave in surprising, sometimes shocking ways. Everyone has some kind of issues with their parents; if they don't have any issues at the start of the planning process, chances are good that they will develop some as the wedding approaches.

Handling these problems becomes the big challenge. They're your *parents*. And they're doing a lot to help you with this wedding. When they lose their minds, act inappropriately, and cause problems, how do you fix that? When you have diplomacy on your side, you can talk to them—not *down* to them—as a problem solver, returning their attention to what's really important: your wedding and your future life with your husband. You already have some terrific skills of your own. You're the one who knows them so well, and you know all of those personal rules about what will work with them and what won't. In this chapter, we'll go through the most commonly reported problems with parents, and you'll get the language and diplomatic choreography to best handle each conflict . . . or at least soften the edges enough to lessen their influence, letting you get back to a place where you can truly enjoy your wedding.

**Q.** In order to plan our wedding day the way we want it, my fiancé and I have decided to pay for the wedding ourselves. We know our parents are expecting to have control over the plans—they're already talking about what they want—so how do we break the news to them that it's going to be our way?

**A.** Many parents simply aren't aware that it's become a big trend—and growing closer to the norm—for brides and grooms to plan and pay for their own weddings. So their long-held expectations of the wedding they'll give you, which they may have thought about on the day you were born, could be deeply entrenched. If they're talking about it now, in the way you described, they're probably going to be pretty stunned that they don't get to have their dream their way. Your fears could start to spin out imaginary scenes of how they'll react and how angry they'll be, but you never know how it will go until you're in the moment. What helps is your great diplomacy in how you tell them. Parents do want to be addressed with respect and gratitude, so it would be best to make sure your speech is filled with positives. Here's your script:

> **YOU:** "Mom, Dad, we can't thank you enough for the engagement present, and it was so exciting to celebrate with you and the family. It was a great way to start this exciting time."
>
> **MOM AND DAD:** "Anything for you, sweetheart."

**YOU:** "We've started thinking about our plans for the wedding, and we've decided that we'd like to pay for the entire thing ourselves."

**MOM AND DAD:** "What?"

**YOU:** "It's something we really feel strongly about, and we've been saving for a while so that we can have the thrill of knowing that we planned our wedding on our own."

**MOM AND DAD:** "Oh, so you don't want our help?" (Arms crossed over chests, eyebrows raised.)

**YOU:** "It's absolutely not that at all. We're looking forward to working with you on things like finding a ballroom, and Mom I'd love for you to come dress shopping with me. And if there's anything else you'd like to join in on, that would be terrific!"

Stay away from leaning too heavily on the "we're just doing this to save you money" angle here, because if parents have the money to spend then they have a leverage tool. If you hold up the money concern torch as the reason you're doing this, they can argue down your reason. Money itself is a loaded issue. Parents might tell you that it's silly (or irresponsible) for you to spend all of your hard-earned money on a wedding when that money could go to a down payment on a house, or to pay off your student loans, and that you'd be better off letting them foot the bills. That money issue is a danger to your diplomacy right now. We all know that weddings are expensive, but that's a flimsy diplomatic tool in this situation. Stick with your excitement about paying for the wedding on your own, as a sense of pride that you're fully able to do so, and mention the specifics of what you'd like your parents to be involved with. That's a very important part of your diplomacy, as it shows your parents that you do value them, and that you're excited to share the wedding planning with them.

## Keeping the Peace

A cut-and-dry "Hey, we're planning everything—sorry to disappoint you" will set off a chain reaction of unpleasant scenarios and sentiments that never had to happen in the first place. If you took a big moment like that and crushed them, it's very much a hit-and-run. And your parents will likely be very hurt that you told them that way.

**Q.** We're planning the wedding with both sets of parents, but the mothers are feuding over every-thing—even the things they didn't originally want to help with. We hate it that they can't work together. Should we fire them now so they don't ruin all chances of a close, harmonious family in the future?

**A.** Of course you want the mothers to get along, and letting them continue to feud over the wedding plans is going to greatly reduce your chance of having an amicable extended family in the future. (Remember, your wedding is important, but your future is more important.) So while firing them isn't the answer—since nothing could be worse for your future than giving these women the boot—you do need to rearrange their situation. This will take some careful diplomacy. They'll both feel that their opinion is the right opinion, they'll resent you for taking sides, and no parent wants to be treated like the petulant child (even if she's acting like one).

Try saying this: "We're going to make some changes in how things are going to get done. I love it that we're all planning the wedding together, and that's going to continue. Just in a different way. Now, you both want to work on the wedding flowers, and I know that you both have different styles and ideas for the centerpieces. So, Mom, you and I will work on the flowers for the ceremony site, since your ideas on roses and gardenias really fit the church. [Mother-in-law], you and I will work on the boutonnieres and the bridesmaids' bouquets. And [fiancé] and I are going to do the centerpieces, since we already have some beautiful ideas."

You're not acting like the boss, and should never talk to your mothers like they're working for you. In any area where they can't be divided, you'll work with them. Or, you and your fiancé will work with them together.

When you have mothers with differing opinions and clashes of personality, take each category of the wedding and spell out precisely what their involvement will be, complimenting them on the ideas they've already shared and expressing gratitude for their involvement.

You're building a custom arrangement, separating the mothers without actually saying that's what you're doing and without insulting them. Your diplomatic tone is one of, "I really want to enjoy working on these things with you." You're putting the focus on sharing the tasks with them, rather than lecturing them on why they can't get along. It takes time for both sides of the family to grow close, and the mothers are operating under intensified emotions right now. So they're doing some primal territory-marking while they're picking out napkin colors. Once you understand that and the mystery is gone, your hurt feelings can turn into forward-thinking diplomacy and you can create just enough distance between them to prevent the fighting and perhaps ease them into a closer working relationship once they have more experience with one another.

If this compromise doesn't work and they're still making it all about themselves, then you can step in with a calm and poised, "We've tried to find a way for this to work, but it's gotten to a point where I don't see a way for us to work on the flowers as a group. Instead, I'm going to arrange everything with the floral designer." Don't throw in a dramatic "on my own!" or "without you!" since you'd open yourself up for criticism. A mother who can't cooperate with another adult on flowers is definitely going to take a shot at you with a quip like, "Oh, you've always been so dramatic," or the other all-time favorite, "Stop being a martyr." Mothers who fight over tulips would stoop to that level. Watch your wording, and stick to the fact that you're now in charge of your own flowers.

Again, this is only if all fair diplomatic efforts have failed. You're not firing them, per se. You're acting in your own best interest to get the flowers you want for your wedding day.

**Q.** My parents are paying for the wedding, and it started off with them respecting my wishes and planning things as I wanted them. Now that more time has passed, my parents are changing some of my plans, saying that their paying for the wedding entitles them to have "just a few things" their way. They're getting power hungry.

**A.** Parents I've spoken to about this very same scenario—and it is a common one—say that they regret losing their perspective and trying to lay claim to the wedding. Since weddings are such emotionally charged events, and because the expense can be so overwhelming, it's very easy for a parent to lose their balance and move into the "me, me, me" zone. As the bride, your best diplomatic move is not to get angry, but to gently lead them back to a better perspective (as they will undoubtedly do for you when you lose your perspective as the wedding approaches). With an understanding of this almost universal phenomenon, you'll be able to handle the problem without making the mistakes that turn this very manageable situation into a relationship-altering power struggle. Here is your script:

YOU: "Mom, Dad, let's talk about the changes you'd like to make to the reception menu."

This opens the door to communication and keeps you all on the topic. As an example of what not to say, consider: "We have to talk about how you said it was going to be our way, and now you're saying you want x, y, and z," which comes off as accusatory and filled with attitude. Your opener just closed the door. Stick with one solid topic, and listen to your parents. Why do they want the changes to the menu?

**MOM AND DAD:** "We just think that Australian lamb would be a little more original, since everyone has chicken and salmon at weddings." That might be what comes back to you, which would reveal that your parents aren't necessarily trying to get things their way, but might genuinely be trying to please everyone more. Be careful not to assign extra meanings to what people suggest.

Now, regardless of whether you're talking about lamb on the menu or gardenias in the centerpieces, here's the diplomatic choreography that gets everything back in line without ruffling feathers. Start by saying: "We just wanted to thank you again for all you're doing to help us create our dream wedding. We're very aware of the prices of everything and how much you're putting into the day, and it means the world to us that we're all able to share the planning process like this." And there you have it. You're expressing the appreciation that anyone would want to hear while doing so much for another person, reminding them of just how precious they are to you, and reaffirming that the focus is on planning your dream wedding. What you'll probably hear is, "It's our pleasure," as opposed to any defensive posturing about what they want their way.

If you have a stubborn case of parental self-centeredness, you'll need to be a little more assertive by saying: "Mom, Dad, we know you're putting a lot into this wedding, and we love you for being so generous to us. At our first meeting, you said you'd do anything to give us the day of our dreams, so we just want to get us all back to that place, with us all excited and planning a wedding that reflects [fiancé] and me." With the look in your eye, they'll know where this is heading. "We've been enjoying incorporating many of your wishes and our family traditions into the day," and mention them specifically, since some people "forget" what they've gotten already. "But you're starting to request more and more of your ideas, and that's making us a little nervous. We feel like the wedding isn't going to reflect us as much as we'd like it to."

You haven't said, "we feel like the wedding is going to reflect you," which may be at the core of your concern. Parents who obviously want a big party with the spotlight on them can renew their wedding vows at another date and time, rather than try to add their long list of wishes to your big day. That's a good suggestion to parents who are really into the planning aspect—they can channel their wishes into their own cele-bration later, and your wedding gets back on track as yours. Try saying: "I've read a lot about the new trend in renew-ing wedding vows, that more couples are having wedding-style celebrations or even small parties at home that they have catered. It's like a mini-wedding do-over. Maybe you and Dad could plan a renewal celebration and use some of these great ideas at your party."

Of course, it's all in the tone. You're being upbeat and positive, not in any way sarcastic ("Use your ideas at your own party!"). Many brides and grooms say that when they mention the idea of a vow renewal, parents' eyes glimmer and they save some of their creative genius for their own personalized parties. The focus then returns, in a more clarified way, on what you want for your wedding.

**Q.** My parents aren't as well-off as my fiancé's parents, and they won't be able to pay for the big, formal wedding that we want. My fiancé's parents have offered to contribute to our wedding fund, and I'm afraid that my parents will be offended or embarrassed about that.

**A.** Many parents take this very seriously, since they have long dreamed about giving their daughter the wedding of her dreams. But the realities of life have dealt their hand, and together with the quickly rising cost of weddings, the parents of the bride might not be able to pay for their daughter's dream wedding. And that's more the norm now, as most weddings are planned by either the bride and groom on their own, or by the bride and groom together with both sets of parents. Since parents might not be completely aware of this trend, it's up to you to tell them, with full diplomacy, that you'll accept your fiancé's family's offer to help pay for the wedding. Here's your script to deliver in person to your parents, if possible, or with both of them on the phone if they live far away: "We've started thinking about the size of the wedding we want, how formal we want it to be, and many of those details. I know that you've offered to pay for the wedding, and we appreciate that so, so much. We know of a lot of couples who wish they had parents who were willing to contribute to their wedding day. We've talked about it, and since we don't feel comfortable having you pay for this big of a wedding on your own, and since we can't contribute more than [dollar amount] on our own, we wanted to let you know that [your fiancé's] parents have offered to contribute as well."

They may jump in here with a "No, that's not how it's done! The bride's parents pay!"

You can respond by saying: "Well, we read that most weddings are planned by the bride and groom together with both sets of parents, so this is the big trend. The majority of weddings are planned this way." Parents who haven't heard of this arrangement may need some additional encouragement.

> **YOU:** "It's going to mean so much more to us, knowing that all of our parents were involved." That sets your standard higher—that it's about working together with your parents, not about their money. And that's the biggest key to diplomacy when it comes to parents and money.

**PARENTS:** "But we're going to look cheap!"

**YOU:** "No, not at all! (Laughing) It's not like we're going to have tags on the gown, the flowers, and the cake saying 'Paid for by. . . .' We're just all contributing what we can to the areas we want to participate in, as full partners."

**PARENTS:** (embarrassment may be setting in here) "What are [your fiancé's] parents going to think of us? I know we're not lawyers like they are. . . ."

**YOU:** "They think you're wonderful! They so enjoyed meeting you at the engagement party." Keep it about the interpersonal relationship, not the money issue. If they haven't met yet, it makes your parents' embarrassment worse with a good dose of fear, since the financial discrepancy has predated their face-to-face meeting. Eliminate this worry with a statement like, "We've told them all about you, and Dad, [your fiancé's] father loves the Knicks too. You're all going to get along so well! Working on this wedding together with them is going to give you a chance to get to know them and bond with them, and we can't wait for that."

There's no need to mention that your fiancé's father has courtside season tickets to the Knicks, and that he offered to bring your dad to a few games, since any display of wealth bragging is the opposite of what you should be doing now. To eliminate your parents' fears, mention only common ground, starting with everyone's joy at working on the wedding together.

Now, what happens if your parents say, "Tell them thanks for the offer, but we'd like to pay for our daughter's wedding on our own"? This automatic comeback may be their response in the moment, and here's where you take that patience characteristic and put it into practice.

Try saying: "Mom, Dad, I know it's important to you to give us a beautiful wedding and that this arrangement has come as a surprise to you. So please just take some time to think about it, since we'd really like to work together with all of you."

Don't give them a time limit. Don't attempt to sway them right now. They just heard something they weren't expecting. Let them sleep on it. And—only if you have to—gently allude to the fact that weddings today cost more than $40,000 on average. You're planning on a guest list of 200 people, so it really would take a lot of pressure off everyone to have more people planning, paying, and enjoying the wedding together. No need to send over a big, imposing dollar amount, since that tactic is going to backfire and make your parents feel even worse about not being able to pay for the wedding you want. Money, again, is not a good diplomatic tool. But a hint of why this group planning team is a benefit to all can help your case.

Finally, complete this open-ended conversation, as your parents consider the offer, with the promise that everyone will get to choose which portions of the wedding they'd like to work on. No one is getting to take over anything—I know from real couples' reports that a common parental fear is that the rich parents will get the reception and that the less wealthy parents will get stuck with the table rentals. You'll all get together for dinner and talk about how the plans will unfold. When you allay their fears, they will lead themselves to a comfortable agreement.

## Keeping the Peace

Money, again, is not a good diplomatic tool. As the plans go on, make it a self-promise that you won't bring the dollar amounts into play. You won't talk with your parents about how much your fiancé's parents are contributing, and you won't talk with his parents about how much your parents are contributing. It's not about the numbers. When you honor the givers and ignore the digits, you'll keep the focus off any comparisons. You are all equals.

**Q.** My parents are strict Catholics, and they're demanding that we have our wedding in their church. We're not connected to that faith, and we'd rather have our wedding outside of a church. My parents are furious and have threatened to not come to the wedding.

**A.** Problems with parents' beliefs are far more complicated than problems with the wedding money. You may find yourselves initially in a situation where the parents have taken a stand as a matter of loyalty to their faith or to a higher power, and there you are trying to figure out why that matters more than their loyalty to you. It can be very upsetting, and it may seem like a no-win situation. Many couples have given in, had their wedding in the church, and resented it for years afterward. That can seem like the only solution when you know your parents, you know how firm they can be in their beliefs, and you know that they really wouldn't show up to your wedding. Some parents have done just that.

Before you find yourselves in a no-win situation like this one, try a new diplomatic approach. Several, if that's what it takes. Go to your parents in person, at a time that you've set aside for a focused discussion on the wedding plans—don't drop by when they're watching TV or have to go out to dinner in an hour. A surprise attack is not going to work here, nor is a forewarning, such as "we're coming over to talk about the whole church thing."

> **YOU:** "We're quite upset that you threatened not to come to the wedding if we don't have the wedding in your church," is your direct opener. You're telling them, and showing them, that their threat hasn't worked effortlessly, that it's hurting you. The degree to which that affects them depends on how fiercely they cling to this decision of theirs.

> **PARENTS:** "Well, you know how much our faith means to us."

**YOU:** "We're not members of your church, and while we respect you and love you for your religious beliefs and values, we would like our wedding to take place in a location that reflects our beliefs and values. We believe we're closer to God when we're outdoors, so that's why we want an outdoor wedding." That presents them with your perspective. You're not planning a heathen wedding with a pig sacrifice.

Or, you may have your eye on a beautiful beach setting, a lovely botanical garden, or your childhood home. When you tell them your wishes calmly and directly, they may hear it fully. They might not have known that your religious beliefs lie in the outdoors, and may have believed all this time that you had no religious or spiritual beliefs at all. Some parents may cling to an "our way or no way" belief system that can be very hard to challenge.

Start by saying to them: "We've been very sure for years that we want to get married at the botanical gardens," which informs your parents that it's your wish to get married at that particular location. Again, that may be news to them. "We had our second date there, and every time we've passed it since, we've always said that's where we're going to get married someday." You're communicating the truth, that this location is an important part of your love story.

While "we've fallen in love with a location" might be your reasoning, it could also be that you simply don't like your parents' church or synagogue. It may be that there's not enough room for your guests, you don't like how they perform ceremonies, the church is not close to your reception hall, or you don't like the officiant's style or personality. When it's a problem with the house of worship in question, this is a challenge to convey to your parents when their church is their second home. Your beliefs could come across like an affront to them. So here is your script:

> **YOU:** "We considered your church, but it's simply not right for us. It's way too massive for our small guest list" (or way too small for your large guest list). "And we understand that the officiant doesn't allow any personalizations to the wedding vows or readings. They don't allow secular music, and other strict rules that would make most of what we want for our ceremony impossible. I know you love your church, but it's simply not going to work for our wedding."

They may argue with you.

> **PARENTS:** "Well, have you *tried* to get some of the rules changed? You haven't even met with [officiant's name]!"

> **YOU:** "We don't want to waste our time or his time. The church doesn't work for us."

A dozen suggestions later, and you might find yourselves still defending your wish. It's now time to make it clear that the house of worship will not be your setting.

**TELL THEM:** "I know this is really important to you, but please keep in mind that the ceremony location has to be important to us. We hope you're not serious about boycotting our wedding," and be sure to use the word "boycotting," since it has such a negative connotation.

Continue on, "If we were to *give in* to your threat not to come to the wedding, and have the wedding in your church," take a breath, "Would that really make you happy? To know that we're unhappy where we are? That it's not a reflection of us? That we're there because you forced us to be there?"

Your parents might absorb this, they might fight you, or they might tell you how this would be a good time for you to re-embrace the religious values they raised you with. That's what they may be hoping for. This doesn't make them bad people. In their way, they're trying to guide you to something they think would be good for you, but they're not understanding that they can't get you to live by their beliefs. This is one symptom of parents who are afraid to let go.

Now you'll present them with the elements of your shared belief system, if there are any, by saying "We're planning on having a minister there, and the ceremony will be based on the traditional scripts. We'll have a reading of [parents' favorite scripture], and the guitarist will play [parents' favorite hymn]. So, you see, we do have some elements of our faith in our planned wedding. These are the things we really want in our ceremony."

## Keeping the Peace

Parents *love* to hear that their advice brought about a great result.

This may or may not register with them. You have no way of knowing how many elements are affecting their decision—pressure from other family members, superstition, and so on—so don't make yourself nuts trying to figure it out. Just express your wishes and your unhappiness with their threat.

Tell them: "We would really like you to be at the wedding, since it would be heartbreaking not to have you there, but we're not going to get married at your church. Please reconsider, and please see that just because we're not going to be in the church doesn't mean that it's not going to reflect our religious and spiritual beliefs."

This is all you can do. Even the best diplomacy can't make others change their minds or be considerate of your feelings, and it can't stop others from making mistakes they'll regret later. Give it your best shot, be honest, keep your anger out of it, and try as many times as possible to express to them how much it means to you that they attend your wedding.

 **My parents think we're getting married too soon.**

**A.** They're just looking out for you, and may be adhering to some belief they have that people get married after X number of years together. Go to them and explain:

> **YOU:** "I just know that we're right together. We have the same beliefs on family, on faith, on money, on children, and I love his family. We're preparing for our future, and we're both very happy. It's not a matter of the number of days we've known each other, but how close we've grown during those days. I hope you'll look at us and see how happy we are, and know as well that this is right."

They might come back at you with their concerns.

> **PARENTS:** "You haven't spent enough time experiencing different life situations!"

> **YOU:** "We're aware that we have a lot of things to face together in the future, but we're committed to one another, and we both know we can handle anything. We have a lot of support in our families and great role models—we have as many advantages as any marrying couple can hope for. So can you please forget about this whole 'too soon' thing and be happy with us?"

Be sure to listen to your parents, though. They may have picked up on some issues that you haven't noticed in your blissed-out engaged status. If they bring up anything specific, like your fiancé's jealousy or how you're not fully yourself when you're with him, these are things for you to think about as you prepare for the wedding and for the future. Your parents' input may be off-base, but devoting some time to looking at it will only show you if you have something to work on, or that you don't have to work on that particular thing. Their concerns could show you how right you are together, which is something to bring up later.

> You can show your concern by saying: "I've been thinking a lot about what you said a few months ago about it being too soon for us to get married. You inspired us to read [book title] and really talk further about important issues like kids and money. I know that you have my best interests at heart, and I love you for speaking up about your concerns. Now we know that we really are doing the right thing by marrying one another. So thank you."

Parents love to hear that their advice brought about a great result.

**Q.** This is my second wedding. I got married when I was twenty-one, and that marriage lasted only two years. Now I'm older, wiser, and getting married again to a far better choice of man. My parents are saying that they won't pay for the wedding because "they already paid for one, and parents don't pay for second weddings." This is my fiancé's first wedding, and I'd really like it to be a dream day. How can I talk some sense into my parents?

**A.** If your parents have decided that they don't want to pay for your wedding, that's their choice. But since you said "parents don't pay for second weddings," make sure your parents aren't holding back from wanting to pay for your wedding because they think there's an etiquette thing holding them back.

Try saying: "While I respect whatever choice you make, please know that there's no etiquette rule saying parents can't be involved in a second wedding. Parents can be involved to any level, and that's something that we can all talk about. We can custom-create this wedding based on whatever you'd like to do."

That opens the door for them to decide, without any force-feeding about how this is your fiancé's first wedding, how they'd like to participate.

**Q.** My parents are newly divorced, and they're using my wedding as a battleground. They're insisting that they both get front row seats at the wedding, but they don't want to share the same row with each other. What can I do?

**A.** Avoid getting sucked down into this battle of the divorced egos, since there will be more problems in addition to this seating dilemma as the wedding approaches. Your best approach is to go to each parent separately, and ask them to keep your happiness in mind.

You can approach them with: "I know that you and [Mom/Dad] aren't getting along, but would you please take one day off from the battle to just be my parents and help make this day extremely happy for all of us? It would mean a lot to me if you would promise—*promise*—to just peacefully coexist for the day, stay away from each other, and enjoy the wedding."

Refrain from delivering any digs about how immature they're being. It's not necessary to point out the obvious. Just focus on what would make everyone happier that day.

As far as the seating for the ceremony, most divorced parents get seated in the front row—since there's room for at least six to ten people in most settings—with or without a neutral party sitting between them.

When it comes to the many additional issues that can crop up as the parents navigate a post-divorce wedding host scenario, welcome their honest approach to you with: "If there's anything else you have concerns about, please feel free to come to me with your requests. I want both you and [Mom/Dad], and your dates, to be comfortable and happy on the wedding day, and we can figure out a solution to any problems."

That right there is brilliant, forward-thinking diplomacy. You've just eliminated a wide range of problems by letting the parents know they don't have to worry or manipulate, try to preempt problems on their own, or worry about offending you with their concerns. You're thinking of everyone's happiness, and you're willing and able to find solutions.

**Q.** My father is bringing his new girlfriend—the one he cheated on my mother with—to the wedding, and my mother is devastated and embarrassed that she will be there. The relatives all know what happened, and my mother doesn't want to be humiliated. How can I best handle this situation?

**A.** Who can blame your mother for not wanting to be humiliated at your wedding? You have a choice—either ask your father not to bring the girlfriend to the wedding, and probably walk right into your father's tirade that it's his right to bring the woman that he loves, or find a way to help your mother out. The girlfriend is going to be a distraction. If the whole family knows what happened, then you'll likely face an initial group look at her, and then everyone will just forget she's in the room. It may become uncomfortable for her to be there, or maybe not. She may be the type to thrive on the controversy she causes. So talk with your father about the situation, and ask what he suggests.

You can say "I'm glad you're happy with [girlfriend], but, thinking about the wedding, I'm very concerned that it's going to be uncomfortable for me and [fiancé] to worry about all the many hurt feelings and negative attention that will be going on."

That's how you put it, mentioning nothing about the girl-friend causing any problems, since he will defend her to thus defend his own choices. No doubt, this girlfriend has already pressured him about this wedding, one way or the other. She may not even want to be there.

Follow up with: "So what can we come up with to make this as comfortable as possible for all of us?" Let your dad suggest a few things, and hopefully he'll be able to focus on your happiness. Then, see if you can diplomatically arrange for some specific things: "We've talked about this, and we would like pictures to be taken separately, seating will be arranged at a distance, and she won't be listed on the pro-gram since you're not married, according to etiquette rules we read in a book."

If he objects, you can be firm by saying: "I know that you want to make [girlfriend] comfortable, but we strongly believe in these arrangements." You're not going to say, "We're thinking of Mom," because that opens a Pandora's box of your father's competitive streak, or the girlfriend's competi-tive streak. Just keep Mom out of this conversation to give yourselves the best chance of good negotiations.

Now for your mother's side: This understandably has her concerned. She doesn't want to relive the hurt and humilia-tion of the betrayal in front of all her family and friends. But here is where you become priceless to her with your diplo-macy and support.

You can say: "Mom, you're going to look beautiful on the wedding day, and you're the host. You're the mother of the bride.

They say the best revenge is being happy, so just walk in there looking like a million bucks, ignore them, have a great time, dance, laugh, and show everyone how great you're doing. It would be a second crime if this situation stole your happiness on the wedding day. We're going to seat you separately from them, so don't worry about that."

With your help, your mother can rise above any spectacle and shine on her own. Let her know that you're here to support her, and that you want her to be happy on the big day.

**Q.** **My mother is using my wedding to compete with her sister and friends. I've heard her bragging on the phone about the wedding they're giving me, and I don't want that to make my relatives or family friends feel badly about the weddings they're planning now. This isn't a competition, and I don't want to be in the game.**

**A.** You're not in the game. Your mother is gabbing about your wedding with her sister and her friends, and you have no idea if people's feelings are being hurt. I know that this concern of yours is because you're a decent, gracious person, and those are wonderful qualities. See your mother's bragging as a limited-time thing, her form of fun, and perhaps her friends' and sisters' form of fun as well. If you'd feel better about saying something, avoid being judgmental (because then you get sucked into the game), and just say, "Let's keep some of the wedding details to ourselves, so that the guests are surprised when they show up. You don't want to give too much away, or they won't be as impressed on the wedding day."

Mom won't want that. Done.

**Q.** My parents are operating under etiquette rules from forty years ago. They're not aware that a lot of etiquette has changed and is not so stiff anymore. I've given them etiquette books and articles to read, but they're sticking to their beliefs that "this is how it should be done." I don't want a stiff, old-world wedding.

**A.** You and your parents have different ideas on how weddings should be done. You've shown them the latest books and articles, and it hasn't made a difference. Your parents are sticking to their belief system. In good diplomacy, you're looking for give-and-take, so sit down with your parents and figure out where you both can give and take.

## Keeping the Peace

Always start with giving them something they want the most.

Try starting with: "You have strong beliefs about wedding etiquette as you understand it, and I have strong beliefs about wedding etiquette as I understand it. But in listening to you"—this is a great phrase to use to show them that you have been listening—"I see that you're very attached to the etiquette of wedding invitation wording. You described it as 'proper,' and I agree with that. So we'll use the traditional etiquette wording of the invitations. But we're not going to do the white card with black print. I know that's how it was done in the past, but today's formal invitations come in beautiful colors, and we definitely want a sage green card with dark green lettering. We read the rules about invitations, and it's the wording that conveys the information to the guests; the style is very much up to us."

You'll go through each etiquette standoff like this, working together with your parents to blend their old-world wishes with your modern-day wishes, in true give-and-take fashion, so that everyone is happy.

**Q.** **My dad wants to walk me down the aisle, but I'm closer to my stepfather, as he is the one who raised me. My mother says I should respect my dad, but I know my stepfather would be very hurt if this near-stranger took over his place.**

**A.** Your feelings are extremely valid, since it's your stepfather who provided you with the fatherly guidance and protection that is symbolized by the "giving away" of a bride. Your mother is trying to do the right thing and take the high road by sparing your biological father's feelings, but the unfortunate side effect of such goodness is a "Which Dad Dilemma." While you feel like you're in a spot where you have to choose, you're actually not. The best approach is to follow the same symbolism. Here is your script, which you'll deliver to your mother, father, and stepfather: "I've been thinking a lot about how I'd like to be escorted down the aisle. I've decided that I'd like my father—who started my life—to escort me halfway up the aisle. That represents my childhood. Then, I'd like [stepfather] to meet me halfway and walk me the rest of the way—representing the later part of my life where he was the guide, the protector, and the provider—to my groom."

Some brides ask their biological fathers to walk alongside them for this part of the journey, since the brides do carry a part of their biological fathers with them (if only in their DNA). But it's the stepfather and mother who say "We do" when asked who gives this woman to this man. No choice is made, no one is left out, no one is hurt. And your gorgeous walk down the aisle honors each man in each stage of your life, ending up with the one who gets your future.

If anyone objects to this very fair and meaningful plan, you can stop that conversation with a simple, "Well, if we can't make this work, then my second option is to walk myself down the aisle on my own. I'm fine with that."

They'll likely agree to Plan A.

**Q.** I'd like both of my parents to walk me down the aisle, but my mother says that's not how things should be done in the church. How can I get her to fulfill my wish to have both parents by my side?

**A.** This is a simple one. Just say: "Mom, this is how a lot of brides are doing it these days, so don't worry about how it's 'done.' I've spoken to the officiant, and he says it's a very common arrangement for the weddings he's done. I'd be honored if you and Dad will walk with me."

**Q.** My mother passed away years ago, and my stepmother has established herself as the host of the wedding. She's unhappy about our plans to do tributes for my mother. How can she be jealous of my departed mother?

**A.** While she might not want to share the spotlight with your departed mother, there could be an element of good intention here that you're not seeing. Maybe she just doesn't want you or anyone else to be sad about your mother not being physically present at the wedding. She might think that tributes would add grief to your day. I'm giving her the benefit of the doubt, which is key to making diplomacy work. It's not very effective when you have anger at what someone is doing. So take a breath and focus on the solution.

Try saying: "[Stepmother's name], I appreciate that you're working so hard to help us plan the wedding," and yes, this is a subtle way of reminding her that she's a helper, not the host. "You've mentioned that we shouldn't do any tributes to my mother, and while I see that as your effort to spare us any sadness on the wedding day, it's very important to me and to my entire family to include my mother in the ceremony in a very special way. So we're going through with the reading, the flower tribute, and the song."

## Keeping the Peace

Giving someone the benefit of the doubt is a key to making diplomacy work.

There's no need to follow up with all of the big moments your stepmother will be getting—as in "Don't worry, you'll get a dance with my father, and your name will be in the program too"—since that implies that you think her problem is jealousy. If it isn't, you've just offended her pretty badly with an assumption. So don't even go there. Just end this topic with your thanks for her great work on the wedding, and change the topic to another category where she's helping out with the plans.

**Q.** My in-laws don't like me. I've tried everything to get them to know me. I'm not disrespectful, and I'm getting tired of jumping through hoops to win them over. I want a harmonious relationship with my in-laws but they're determined not to like me. My fiancé is turning it on me, saying that I'm too sensitive.

**A.** Infuriating, isn't it? Not only does the family have preconceived ideas about you, but your fiancé isn't standing up for you or supporting your benevolent goal to have a harmonious relationship with them. There is no confrontation that will solve this, no magic words or Hallmark moment that will turn your group into a close-knit family just yet. So keep up your efforts to get to know them, let them get to know you, and allow time and good experiences to bring you together. In the movie The Family Stone, Sarah Jessica Parker's character Meredith practically kills herself jumping through hoops to get her fiancé's family to like her, but she's scared and uptight about it, which leads to blunders that undermine her goals. So lighten up, do less to accomplish more, and preface this new method of yours with a great diplomatic conversation with his parents.

"[Your fiancé] has told me how much he loves being a part of this family, and I love him for the values he got from you. I know I'm not what you expected for his fiancée, but I hope you'll grow to know me, then to like me, then to love me, since I'd like nothing more than to be welcome in your family, to share some of what made [fiancé] the amazing man that he is, and bring whatever I can to your family."

Then follow those words up with actions over time . . . cook for them, share family holidays (families hate it when you demand that every holiday be spent with your family, where you're more comfortable during this adjustment phase), and—most important—show them how much you love their son. Actions speak loudest. Give it time, as diplomacy in this scenario needs time to take root.

**Q.** My father isn't a very pleasant man, and he keeps making negative comments about marriage and about my fiancé. I'm very nervous that he's going to say something to embarrass me in front of my in-laws on the wedding day.

**A.** He probably will, and many brides have survived exactly this kind of embarrassment. His words and actions reflect on him, and if you were to say, "Now Dad, don't say anything embarrassing," guess what's going to happen? Some fathers are able to respect their daughters' wishes, and others are less like fathers and more like mean-spirited schoolyard bullies who want you to be afraid. Asking them to behave, when their character leads them to say such negative things, could lead to a barrage of just what you don't want. So save your diplomacy for the moment. When Dad says something goofy just to cause trouble or in a pathetic attempt for a laugh, just smile, shake your head, and let it roll off your back with a comment of, "I got Mom's sense of humor," or "Good one, Dad" right before you seamlessly and calmly change the subject.

If your father says something disparaging about marriage, your response should be, "Well, I don't agree with that," instead of an emotional outburst. It takes strength to breathe your way through such horrific moments, grace to step aside from them and let them float away, and a supportive fiancé to let you vent your emotions later. Your father has some issues, and they're not yours to solve.

## Keeping the Peace

Your best diplomacy is to make each moment enjoyable despite the negative influence of others.

**Q.** My parents promised that they'd pay for certain parts of the wedding, and we booked the experts we wanted. Now that the wedding day is closer, my parents are saying that they're short on cash and won't be able to pay for what we've chosen. We know we can't go back in time and not spend money we don't have, but we trusted our parents' word. We can't afford the experts, and we don't want to lose our deposits. How can we get my parents to fulfill their promises?

**A.** Talk to them about this situation, and how you've already booked the experts. Be calm and understanding. Here is your script:

**YOU:** "Mom, Dad, has something happened that has taken up a portion of the family budget?" You're showing empathy first, rather than pursuing the money you were originally promised.

**THEM:** "We originally thought we'd cash in an invest-ment to pay for the wedding, but our business didn't have a great year. So we can only contribute [amount] to the wedding."

Once you're sure there's no big family crisis at hand, like a health problem that will require thousands of dol-lars for doctors' bills, look for ways to get the money that you need to keep your experts, or you may need to play with your wedding budget.

**YOU:** "Okay, let's see what we can do with [amount], where we can still use our vendors. Let's sit down on Sunday and see what we can come up with."

Your parents will be so grateful about your flexibility, as well as your creativity when your Sunday meeting brings your ideas for additional ways to increase your budget. This is when you might suggest that you and your fiancé, or your fiancé's family, can pick up the remaining amount,

Find a new plan, rather than attempt to get your parents to give money they don't want to give. "But you promised!" is an appropriate line for a seven-year-old who didn't get a pony for her birthday, but, as an adult, you're looking for the solution. Understand that most parents don't really know the true prices of wedding services and packages when they first volunteer to help. Prices have skyrocketed in the past ten years alone, so they may have thought that $3,000 can buy a gorgeous wedding when it barely buys a dress. Consider the possibility that they don't feel very good about not being able to give more money, and work with them to come up with less expensive alternatives in your plans. Maybe they know someone who can get you a break on your photography bill. Just because they're not handing over a platinum card doesn't mean their input doesn't have value.

When you take this approach, you become a pricelessly diplomatic member of your own wedding team.

**Q.** I promised my mother that she could come gown shopping with me, but she's been so critical of my weight and my appearance lately. She says she's just trying to help me reach my goal weight for the wedding, but I expect major stress when we do go gown shopping. I don't want to leave her out, but I don't want my gown shopping trip to be a nightmare.

**A.** You have to be direct about your concerns, since gown shopping is a very important, emotional, and sentimental event. You'll always remember it, and to do it justice you want to make sure that everyone involved is completely supportive so that the experience is enjoyable. It's understandable that you're nervous about what your mother might say or do, so your diplomatic approach needs to start with honesty.

You can say: "Mom, I know that you mean well, and you're just trying to motivate me with your comments about my weight. But I have to tell you that when you say things like 'You're going to look huge in that wedding gown' or 'If you eat that cake, you're going to have to wear a size 20,' it hurts me to the core. It's not supportive, and it doesn't motivate me to work on my fitness goals." This may be news to her, because she may think she can shame you into success—people tend to do what they think will work. "To tell you the truth, I'm thinking about going gown shopping without you because I'm afraid that you're going to be critical of how I look, and I just can't have that kind of negative input at such an important event that I've been looking forward to for so long. So here's the deal . . . I need you to promise me that you won't say anything critical about my weight or my appearance during the gown shopping trip—in fact, I'd like you to stop doing that period. I've been very tolerant in the past and then devastated afterward, and I'm very tired of that. Will you promise me that you'll be supportive during the dress shopping trip? I'm very serious about this."

If she promises, wonderful. You have a good chance that she'll abide by your wishes. She may slip and let out a critique if that's her nature, at which point you warn her with a look and a reminder: "Mom, you promised."

Or, she'll tell you that you're being too sensitive, or that you're just cranky because you're failing at your weight goals. Some mothers have come out with such hideous things. If that happens, you leave her out of the shopping trip by simply not inviting her, and that's a life lesson for her.

If she's at the gown shop with you and lets criticism fly, you'll end the session with a statement of, "Thank you, but I'm done for today," make a new appointment for yourself, leave calmly, and return with your maid of honor and a few bridesmaids. Many brides do go on multiple gown shopping excursions before they find the right dress, and since your mother showed she cannot be trusted to refrain from critiques, you'll invite only your closest, most supportive friends and sisters to future shopping trips.

## Keeping the Peace

You've been very respectful and diplomatic, and sometimes you have to take the hard stand to get a message through to a difficult parent.

**Q.** We'd like to have a destination wedding, but my mother is afraid to fly. She's all but begged us to have the wedding in her hometown, which is not our style at all. I understand and sympathize with her fear, but this is our wedding. We'd really love to have it on an island.

**A.** The trend in destination weddings requires key players to travel, which often involves flying. If you decide to keep your plans instead of changing them to accommodate your mother (and some couples do choose this change, figuring they can fly to the island for their honeymoon), then be supportive of the hard work your mother will need to do to attend your wedding.

You can start by saying: "Mom, I know you hate flying, so here are some ideas that can help out with that. We love you and want you at the wedding, and we're going to do everything we can to help get you there."

And that's where you inform her about cruise ships that go to your location, antianxiety medicines that help millions of people fly with little or no fear, exposure therapy, books on overcoming flying phobias, or even a short flight to a resort for a pre-wedding getaway just to give Mom some confidence for the flight over water. Never push, just offer, always reminding Mom that you know she can do it, and you appreciate how hard she's working on overcoming this fear. Some people limit their lives to avoid facing a fear. Your mom is being brave in working on hers.

Another option—more consideration than diplomacy—is choosing an island that can be reached by car. The Florida Keys, for instance, have bridges connecting them, as does Hilton Head Island in South Carolina. Your diplomacy, then, might be in choosing a more accessible island.

**Q.** My mother is a homemaker while my fiancé's mother works a corporate job and travels a lot for work. My mom keeps trying to take planning tasks away from his mother, saying "she doesn't have time," which is making his mother feel judged and left out. She's doing the best she can, so how can I get my mother to stop railroading her?

**A.** This one sounds complicated, with the mother-status elements, but it's really just a matter of saying, "Mom, please don't assume that [fiancé's] mother can't handle the wedding tasks. She's doing a terrific job on every thing she's taken on, and we're very pleased with all she's doing. It's very important to us that she share the planning process with us, and while we know you're just trying to help, and that you're excited, we'd like you to stop offering to take on some of her tasks." The last part is very important wording. You haven't said, "stop trying to take over her tasks," since that's an accusation of a mom-versus-mom showdown, which would only complicate matters further.

## Keeping the Peace

Good diplomacy requires careful word choice and solution-seeking, mixed with compliments and validation for what's going well in action and intention.

**Q.** My parents are telling some of our guests that they should stay in the "nicer" hotel where the wedding will be, and other guests to stay in the budget hotel. They say they're just being considerate, but people are getting offended.

**A.** Yikes—they're trying to help but creating a problem. Stop them now with a simple, "Thank you for trying to help with suggestions on the hotels in the area, but we included hotel cards with the invitation so that guests can make their own choices for themselves. We also added to our Web site that guests can contact us with any questions on the hotels. So there's no need to try to help the guests further with that. Thanks." Then move on to what they can help out with.

**Q.** **My mother is obsessed with the wedding and calls me twenty times a day with new ideas. The wedding is more than a year away, and I don't know how to tell her to back off.**

**A.** Okay, she's overexcited. You know that she doesn't have bad intentions, so your diplomacy is much easier on this one than on most of the other problems in this book. It's just going to be a matter of finding the right way to tell her to rein it in.

Try saying: "Mom, I'm thrilled that you're so excited about the wedding and that you have so many great ideas. But I have to tell you that getting twenty calls a day is starting to overwhelm me, and I'm getting stressed out and feeling like we have to plan this entire wedding in a week. We have a year, so I'd like to take my time, really enjoy the process, and spread out when and how we tackle each category of the wedding. So here's what I suggest: When you get an idea or have a question, write it down in a notebook. Then we'll get together for lunch every now and then to go through everything. I think that would be much more fun, don't you?"

Your mother will see an opportunity here—an even better chance to connect with you over lunch than she has gotten through calling you every day. The way you've explained your desired solution is going to give her what her twenty calls a day were designed for: a bond with you, and the excitement of working on the wedding.

## Keeping the Peace

A habit takes a bunch of attempts to break, so be understanding about her adjusting to your timing request.

She may forget and those calls might start coming in when she loses perspective and something seems urgent. That's absolutely fine from time to time—Mom shouldn't be relegated solely to the weekend meetings, and you may find that her occasional calls during a hectic day boost your enthusiasm level about the wedding. But if she's calling too often again, remind her to just write it down, and you'll talk it all over with her at lunch.

**Q.** **My mother is taking a big chunk of the wedding budget and using it on her gown, shoes, and accessories, plus her hotel room. She's spending more on her gown than I am on mine. She's paying for the wedding, so how do I tell her that we need more**

**of that money for the wedding cake, flowers, and my gown?**

**A.** Be direct. Here's your script:

**YOU:** "Mom, I noticed that you shifted a big chunk of the wedding budget toward your outfit and hotel room, and we haven't ordered the flowers, the cake, or my gown yet. So can we get together to rework the budget, make sure we're clear on how much will be needed for the cake, gown, and flowers before we get into other things?"

Your directness is a positive diplomacy move. You haven't accused her of being selfish, of wanting Manolos and thus forcing you to buy your gown at a garage sale. If her motives are pure, she may respond with:

**MOM:** "You only get married once, sweetheart, and I was just trying to make the most of it. It's only $1,000, after all."

**YOU:** "I completely understand, and I do want you to make the most of it. That's why I'd love to meet and work on the budget so that once we arrange for the cake, the caterer, the flowers, the photographer, and other things, we can see just how much splurge money will be left over." Don't add "for you to spend on yourself," no matter how tempting it might be to say that.

Just stick to the business of the budget, and talk about adjusting the numbers to reflect your highest priority items. It helps to start the process by starring your gown, cake, and flowers as your top priority items, or getting to that step now when it seems like Mom is looking to spend mightily on her own choices.

Of course, Mom might be a little bit more aggressive. She might say, "I'm paying for the wedding, and I want a nice gown. You're already getting [dollar amount] for the wedding, so stop being selfish."

Yes, she just turned it around on you, since she knows she's out of line. People do that when they're busted. Don't take the bait. Just tell her again that you'd like to meet to go over the priority list of your budget. If she's already purchased her items, you're going to have to find other areas of the wedding budget to cut back on. And it's not going to be the cake, gown, or flowers. So Mom's dress, shoes, and hotel room just might have knocked her wish for custom invitations out of the loop.

Finish by saying: "Okay, but I'm just working out what's left in the budget. Given the cost of the flowers, the caterer, and all of the wedding essentials, plus your gown, shoes, and hotel bill, we're no longer going to be able to do the custom invitations you requested." And use the word "requested." This subtle reminder works better than "the invitations you *wanted*." "The invitations I found for less will be just fine," is all the response you need. It's no use to try to shame her about her shoes or teach her a lesson. Just deal with finding a solution to the matter at hand.

**Q.** Both of our parents are divorced and remarried, and they all want to be on the invitation. It would be a big, long list of parents and spouses, and it would overpower our invitation.

**A.** Don't worry about overpowering the invitation, since today's styles of formal invitations now come in square tri-folds and booklet forms for the express purpose of listing all of the parents' names without everything being jammed onto a single-panel card. So look at invitation etiquette books and Web sites to get the correct order of names, and give them their own page or panel on the invitation. Leaving parents' names off the invitation when they're the hosts of the event is one of the worst etiquette mistakes you can make. It's hideously disrespectful to parents who have given you so much, and a disappointment to your fiancé's parents, even if they're not paying for the wedding.

So, your diplomatic solution here is to choose an invitation shape and design that allows plenty of room to honor all of the parents.

**Q.** My mother is upset about how she looks compared to my dad's new wife, and she won't even go gown shopping.

**A.** She's avoiding her image. Here is your script:

**YOU:** "What kind of dress would make you feel most comfortable, Mom? Would you like me to help you find a stylish designer?" She might not be aware that there are so many designers who create fabulous plus-size dresses. Make it easy on her with, "Would you prefer to look at Web sites, rather than go to a dress shop and try on gowns in front of a three-way mirror with a pushy saleslady barging into your dressing room?"

**MOM:** (eyes brightening) "Yes! I absolutely hate going through the racks of dresses and seeing so many ugly gowns for the mother of the bride."

Aha! It wasn't her body image at all. She just hates the *process* of shopping for her gown when she hasn't found a source for pretty gowns, so she was avoiding the image of herself in hideous, sequined monstrosities.

**YOU:** "Mom, there are lots of gorgeous dresses out there, in beautiful colors, so what do you think about going to a department store to have a personal shopper pick out great dresses that are custom-selected according to your style and color wishes? It's like the royal treatment."

Use your diplomacy to find a different way for her to shop for gowns. She doesn't feel as beautiful as the new wife, so she's figuring, "Why bother?" But you can use your enthusiasm to encourage her to start looking in the way that's most comfortable for her. She can, after all, order dresses online and return them if they don't fit. A personal stylist can be hired to come to her house, measure her and talk about her favorite colors and fabrics, or show her how a bolero jacket will make her chest look bigger and her waist look smaller—something she never knew. It just takes your gentle encouragement and suggestions on how to find something she's comfortable with.

Saying "Tell me what you'd most enjoy," is a good way to start. "Even if you're trying on gowns in your bedroom, I want to be there to see how beautiful you look."

Don't bother trying to pump up her ego by saying she's going to look so much better than the new wife. Comparisons aren't a part of good diplomacy. And showering her with compliments could backfire if she doesn't feel that they're sincere. Find the little things she likes and support her as she goes along, letting her know exactly what you love about each dress and which features of hers look terrific in each one, then plan a separate outing to shop for fabulous shoes and accessories. She will love it that you're investing time in helping her.

**Q.** I'd like my parents to give a toast at the wedding, but they say that isn't done.

**A.** Let them know that it is a trend for the parents to give a toast by saying: "Anyone can give a toast at the wedding, and more parents are taking a moment to say a few words as the hosts of the wedding. It's up to you, though. If you'd rather not, that's fine. If you'd rather say a few words at the rehearsal dinner, that would be terrific. Just let us know what works best for you."

You've let them know you like the idea, but you've diplomatically left the choice up to them. No one should ever be forced to speak. And people do get inspired in the moment, so a "No" now might turn into a "Yes" later. You never know.

**Q.** We have a family tribute table with pictures of our relatives' weddings. Since my parents are divorced and both have remarried, how do I handle whether or not to include their original wedding photo? It seems wrong to leave them out. And their new wedding photos would be weird for both of my parents to see, right?

**A.** Again, be direct. Go to them separately and explain your wishes.

**YOU:** "We're setting up our family tribute table with photos from all the relatives' weddings, and I'd like to find out how you feel about including your wedding photo with [Mom/Dad], along with your wedding photo with [new partner]. We don't want anyone to be uncomfortable with either photo being out there, so please let me know if you're okay with our having all three photos displayed."

**MOM/DAD:** "Three? You mean [your mother's/your father's] new wedding photo will be displayed as well?"

They're not being selfish. This is a common reaction to the unexpected. You simply respond, "Yes." No need to explain about being fair to [Mom's/Dad's] new partner. That can be left unsaid.

## Keeping the Peace

Mix in lots of non-wedding photos so that it doesn't seem glaringly obviously that Dad's photo from a football game is the only non-wedding photo on the table while everyone else has a formal wedding portrait.

Your parents might not have a problem with it, and you might not need any diplomacy if there is no problem. If either parent has a problem with it, it doesn't get placed on the table. Use fun family photos instead of wedding photos, such as pictures from your family vacations, photos of your parents with you when you were both babies, and so on. These are big family moment photos and can be even more meaningful on the family tribute table.

**Q.** Our parents gave us a generous amount of money for our wedding plans, but we've run out. How

do we ask for more without seeming greedy or irresponsible with the amount they gave us?

**A.** Asking for more money when parents have already
been generous is one of those ultra-delicate things since there
is a very real risk of seeming greedy or irresponsible with the
money they gave you. To give yourselves an edge, come prepared with a breakdown of where the money they gave you
already went—what you spent on the photographer's package (plus the brochures that show the more expensive packages you didn't take), the limousines, the gown, and more.
And show them the averages of what things cost in your area,
courtesy of the survey results at *www.costofwedding.com*. When
you can back up your request with evidence of why you need
more cash, you're being responsible and respectful of how
they'll feel about your request. Here's what you say: "Mom,
Dad, we absolutely hate coming to you about this," so true,
"but our wedding budget is stretched paper-thin, and we still
have some more necessities to get. So would you consider
giving us [dollar amount] more for our wedding? We can
rearrange our budget some more, but that extra money would
really help us out." You've been honest and direct, which is all
you can do.

Your appreciation has to shine here, not as manipulation but
as a healthy part of diplomacy. You're not a taker, and you're
hoping—not demanding. Never launch into what they gave a
sibling for that wedding, or what other friends' parents gave

them. You've already gotten a lot, so this request is completely at their discretion. They might not have extra money to give you.

If the answer is no, then say, "Okay, thank you. We completely understand." No more, no less, no apologizing for even asking, no second (or third) attempts at swaying them. You'll then devote yourselves to shaving your budget down, getting rid of your lower-priority items, or looking into your own finances to make up the difference. Go back to page 11 for more on bringing your fiancé's parents into the planning process, not as a punishment to your parents, but as a necessity. Weddings *are* obscenely expensive, and you're just trying your best to make your dreams come true.

And honor your parents every step of the way if they're generous enough to help you. Remember, some brides and grooms don't get financial boosts from their parents. Your gratitude needs to be very evident either way.

**Q.** My wedding is all about spring: pink and green, peonies and sweet peas, and so on. I've tried not to be a control freak about what my parents wear, but my mom bought a dress that goes completely against our color scheme. How do I tell her I'd like her in something more in line with our colors?

**A.** First, make sure you're not overreacting to her color choice. If you've chosen pink and spring green and she is in a deeper rose color, then that works. But if she's in black or a wintry cranberry, and you truly fear a clash of hue, you have to approach her with some delicacy:

"Mom, while this dress is really pretty on you, it doesn't coordinate with the colors we're all wearing. It's very important to me that we coordinate at the wedding and in the photos, so can you find another use for this black dress and join me for a dress shopping trip to find another gown?"

It's better to praise the dress first, and then offer a solution for her. Finding another use for the dress is your best first suggestion, since some mothers get offended by the bride's implication that her choice of dress is unwearable or that she only deserves to have one nice dress. I know this is ridiculous, but somehow this is all your mother will hear if you only suggest that she return the dress. Here is your script:

MOM: "But this one looks so great with my skin tone. The woman at the dress shop said so."

YOU: "And she's right. The dress is gorgeous, but it's not right for the wedding. I'd really like for you to wear something in a lighter pink, which also looks great on you."

You've shifted the focus away from what to do with the clashing gown—which is, after all, your mother's choice—and you're moving the issue into the action step.

YOU: "[Department store] has a sale next weekend, so why don't we go see what they have?"

53

And here's where the money will come in.

**MOM:** "But I paid $300 for this dress!"

**YOU:** "Money well spent! It's beautiful, and I'm sure you'll have other events to wear it to, right?"

**MOM:** "Not really. I guess I'll just return it."

Mom just solved her own problem.

**YOU:** "If you want to return it, I'd like to pay for the return shipping, since this was my issue."

**MOM:** "You don't have to."

**YOU:** "I insist."

You've done a terrific thing by offering. From here, you can show Mom some magazine ads or Web site pages featuring the color and formality of gown you'd like her to wear. And make that dress shopping trip an event—take Mom to lunch for being so agreeable with your request.

## Keeping the Peace

Always know the right person for the discussion. Maybe the kid sister can always sway Dad's opinion, or, maybe Mom's adept at getting things done. It's good diplomacy to put the right team member on the task.

**Q.** My father refuses to wear a tuxedo—he says he's not in the wedding party so he shouldn't have to wear one. But my future father-in-law is wearing one, so my dad is going to stand out in the pictures. How can I get him to change his mind?

**A.** First, find out what's on your dad's mind. If he's operating under old-world rules of wedding attire, he's probably been to many weddings over the years where the father didn't wear a tux.

**YOU:** "Actually, it's quite common for the fathers to wear tuxedoes at weddings, and [fiancé's] father is renting one for the wedding. We're planning to have group family photos, and it would look so much better if you were wearing a tuxedo as well."

**DAD:** "So I have to wear one if he's wearing one?"

**YOU:** "We'd really like you to."

You haven't engaged in a competition issue.

**DAD:** "Tuxedoes cost a lot of money to rent."

**YOU:** "Don't worry about that. The tux shop is offering us a free rental with our ten orders, and we'd like you to take that one since you're paying for so much of the wedding."

This offer only works if you've previously cleared it with your fiancé, though. He might have been expecting the freebie for himself. If you can't entice Dad with a free tux offer, then try this: "It's really not that expensive. We've gotten a discount for our large group order, and it's only going to be [amount]. That's far less than what a new suit would cost."

You know how to talk to your dad in his language. If it's a money thing, you know how to show him all the reasons the tuxedo is a good deal. If it's a stubbornness thing, then this is one issue that you can delegate to your mother. She may know how best to talk to him.

# Chapter 2

# The Bridesmaid from Hell

From choosing who is named as a bridesmaid (and who isn't), to handling bitter and jealous bridesmaids, to figuring out how to get such different women to work well together, the ladies of your inner circle can present some tough diplomacy issues. This chapter explores the most commonly reported bridesmaid challenges, all the while understanding that many of these challenges are very much colored by the relationships you have with these women. They're in a position of honor, chosen by you, and they have responsibilities to fulfill for the wedding . . . but they're also your sisters and your friends. So when you apply good diplomacy—even when you'd rather scream at the unnecessary stress they can cause—you're investing in your wedding as well as your future happiness with them in your life.

**Q.** I'd like to keep my bridal party on the small side, and this is a huge problem because I've been a bridesmaid in at least a dozen friends' weddings over the years. Can I only choose my closest friends, and leave out those who I'm not as close to anymore? I'm afraid they'll be hurt not to be included.

**A.** This scenario is quite a common one for brides who have been loved enough to be included in lots of bridal parties. Your list may be a long one, and you may feel like you have to "repay" these friends by including them in your bridal party. But, as difficult as it is to think about it this way, naming someone to a bridal party isn't a transactional arrangement. When someone has a baby and has to name a godparent or guardian, they don't name all of the people for whose children they serve as godparent or guardian. Choices have to be made in life, and these should be made based on the current closeness of the relationship. While you can have as large a bridal party as you wish (see the next entry), you're also free to keep the size of your bridal party small and include only those friends who are closest to you and your fiancé. Your distant friends are very aware that your friendship has faded a little bit, and they know it's not because of a lack of love.

The key to this one is to invite your chosen bridesmaids into your lineup, and enjoy that process. Don't let your fear of what everyone else might think dampen your excitement. You never know . . . some of your more distant friends might not be disappointed not to be named to your bridal party. After all, being in a bridal party entails a lot of work and expense, travel, and long-distance planning, all of which they might be doing for other bridal parties that they're currently in. Most adults are fine with accepting your choices and dealing with any twinges of disappointment.

Your biggest question might be, "Should I tell them ahead of time, or should I just not say anything?" That's the big diplomacy challenge. Your first instinct might be to be open and clear with them, to make sure they're not upset. You don't want to look like you're hiding the fact that you didn't choose them. But wouldn't it be weird to call them up to tell them they didn't make the cut? Isn't that inviting disaster and confrontation?

In this situation, it's best to avoid making the "I just wanted to let you know that you're not in the bridal party" call. Yes, you want to be open and honest, to make sure they don't hear it from others, and to preempt any hurt feelings, but this is too strange a phone call to make. It comes off very much as you trying to assuage your own guilt and fears. Your friends might find it strange that you haven't called in months, and now you call with this. You come off as seeking their validation so that you can feel better. Sometimes honesty has a strange side effect; Your intentions are good, but it doesn't go over well.

If you don't call them, they'll receive a save the date card or an invitation, and since they haven't been asked to be in the bridal party by now, they'll get the message that they're not in the bridal party. And, again, it might be no big deal. If they do contact you with upset feelings about your choice, here's what you can say: "I'm very sorry that you're upset. It was really hard for us to keep our bridal party to a manageable size, after both of our sisters and sisters-in-law, and we weren't able to include a lot of friends we really wanted." Don't go into any offer to give them a special role at the wedding, like greeter or program distributor, because at this point it could feel like a consolation prize. If you want them to have a separate honor position, ask them later. First, spend some time e-mailing with them, refreshing your friendship a little bit, and showing value to the friendship across the miles. Being named to a bridal party isn't the big thing that everyone makes it out to be, but the entire issue makes you evaluate your friendships and reconnect more. It's thinking about the future and the friends who will be in it.

**Q.** I've only just met my fiancé's sisters, and I feel pressured to include them as bridesmaids for the sake of family harmony. That would mean bumping a few of my friends to make room for them in the bridal party lineup, or enlarging our bridal party to a ridiculous size.

**A.** There's no such thing as a ridiculous size for a bridal party. As the bride, you can have any size of bridal party that you'd like. Don't pay any attention to surveys that say six is the top number of bridesmaids you can have, and don't listen to people who warn you that a certain number is too many. Today's bridal party members like being in big groups, since the shower expenses will be more manageable per person and your photos show a great big group of loved ones. Not to mention you'll have a large circle of friends and sisters around you on your big day. So spare yourself the diplomacy problems of leaving out your fiancé's sisters—wouldn't your future mother-in-law be hurt by this decision, and wouldn't the sisters be disappointed to be left out?—and include as many people as you wish. It's your bridal party to plan, which means that his sisters could also stand on his side of the bridal party.

**Q.** I'm not close with my sister at all. We've had a lot of problems over the years, and now she's demanding to be my maid of honor. I'd like to leave her out and have my best friend be maid of honor, but that would really upset my parents. How can I choose between what I want to do and what I should do?

**A.** In the world of weddings, there's a huge undercurrent of family diplomacy. Your decisions now go way beyond the wedding day, and create lasting issues in the family that can arise in the future. I wish it was always as simple as "Do what you want to do, and don't care what other people think," but that's what criminals and other unsavory characters do. It will be best for you to keep the future in mind. So, while leaving your sister out of the bridal party may feel like the right thing to do now, you said it's going to upset your parents. And that will color everything from the wedding plans to family holidays to future events . . . and you know your sister is going to play this up for all it's worth.

So as a matter of forward-thinking diplomacy, consider having your sister as a maid of honor together with your best friend. Brides have two, three, even four honor attendants, since today's weddings allow plenty of room for personalizing to reflect their deepest values. You'll have given the sister a position in the bridal party, which eliminates future family strife, but you can have your best friend be the one who stands next to you, holds your bouquet, and all the other highly meaningful actions for your ceremony. Practice good diplomacy with your sister, a peaceful coexistence, and make a concerted effort to find harmless tasks of honor for her to do. Don't assign her anything from your highest priority level, since it sounds like she might be the type to be controlling about her given responsibilities just to give you a hard time. I wouldn't leave her out of the dress shopping trip, for instance, in any way giving her a message of "Yes, I named you to the bridal party, but I'm not including you in anything else" since that's just playing down on a low level, and it's not becoming of any gracious bride. You'll be proud of yourself for taking the high road, and you'll never know the everlasting fallout from your family that you would have experienced if you left her out. As for her behavior—that's a reflection on her.

**Q.** **In the excitement of the moment when I got engaged, I asked lots of my friends to be bridesmaids and they all said yes. Now that I'm more rational, I**

**realize I made a mistake in asking some of them to be in my lineup. Is there a way to uninvite a few?**

**A.** This happens more often than you might think. In the sheer excitement of an engagement, brides ride a wave of adrenaline that encourages a lot of promises. "Sure! You can get ordained for the day and perform our ceremony!" and "Sure, everyone can bring their kids to the wedding!" are among the other in-the-moment announcements that get a second thought later. Luckily, you're not stuck with fifty bridesmaids and the bartender as your officiant. You can uninvite the extra bridesmaids by saying, "[Fiancé] and I have started with the wedding plans, and while I know that I invited dozens of people to be in our bridal party that night, among many other things I said we'd do, we still have to talk about how large a bridal party we want, whether to include his stepsisters, and on and on. Please forgive me for getting your hopes up. I spoke too soon and I really don't want to make anything official until he and I discuss everything further. We're not sure if we're having a big wedding, or if we're just going to do a destination wedding . . . nothing's set yet. I'm very sorry for this."

The friends' responses are going to depend on their own characters and how much they needed to be included in the bridal party. Most will understand, probably having spoken too soon about something in their lifetimes, and some may be offended. All you can do is apologize and say that you hope they understand.

Do yourself a favor and don't say anything about "We'll let you know if you can be a bridesmaid," as a way to try to be nice or protect someone's feelings. Some people will wait to hear, and it will become a big issue with suspense as to whether or not you find them worthy.

## Keeping the Peace

A big part of diplomacy is knowing when to stop talking.

**Q.** **My friend is very unhappily single, and she seems to resent my engaged bliss. She's being very pouty and not returning my calls, and rolling her eyes when I talk about the wedding. I understand how miserable she is at being one of the only single women in our group, but she's really upsetting me.**

**A.** Your friend might resent your engaged bliss, she might just be after attention, or she might have a personal problem going on. The important thing is not to try to figure out the reason for her behavior, but to go straight for the solution. Create your diplomatic approach with that in mind. Meeting in person is best so that your words are supported by the kinds of body language that show your sincerity, like a hug. Try saying, "[Her name], it feels like we have some distance in our relationship lately, and I'd really like for us to work out whatever we have to." You haven't said anything about her eye-rolling, and you haven't put her on the defensive by saying "I'd really like for us to talk about whatever problem you're having." It's not necessary to say that. You're focused on a solution. She may open up and admit to feeling left out of your excitement, hopeless about ever finding a great guy, or hurt that you haven't spent time with her. Or, she may say that nothing is wrong. In that case, "You're not being yourself lately . . . is everything okay?" is a great, diplomatic friendship expression that opens the door to letting her choose whether she will open up to you.

If she does not open up to you, but rather slaps on a fake smile during your talk only to return to her eye-rolling later, then these are her issues to deal with. It might be that she is having a personal problem, but doesn't want to bring you down or for the news to get out. It could be any number of things. But if you value her friendship aside from this behavior, you'll show that value to her by your presence. Too many brides make the mistake of getting angry or accusing the friend of being selfish or dramatic, which only escalates the problem and ripples outward to other people. Give yourself the best chance of a solution by being a good friend and asking what you both can do to return your relationship to normal.

**Q.** My sister is engaged, and she's using our weddings to compete with me. Everything has to be bigger or better, or she races me to book the same experts I have in mind. How can I get her to stop the sibling rivalry? Our weddings are not a game.

**A.** If your sister has this kind of immaturity in her system, there's very little that you can say diplomatically to eliminate this conflict. Let her drive herself crazy trying to outdo you while you very diplomatically let her competition just roll off your back and continue to enjoy the process of planning your own wedding. If she gets frustrated at not being able to engage you in competition—thus ruining her fun—and becomes rude, your diplomatic response is, "I'd really rather you not talk to me like that." Don't get drawn into her drama. Seek out better-adjusted people to share your excitement with, and don't tell your sister anything about your plans or vendors until after you've booked them with a deposit.

**Q.** My friends do not like my fiancé. I know he didn't make a good first impression, but they're not making the effort to get to know him. I'd really like for them to be excited about our wedding, because it seems like they're not very happy for me.

**A.** You need to tell them exactly that. "Look, I know that [groom] isn't your favorite person. But he's my favorite person, and I really would like you to give him a clean slate and get to know him better. It's causing me a lot of stress to see you guys rolling your eyes at everything he says, and I've talked to him about behaving better with you. So I'm asking you to give me the gift of a fresh start with him, and I'm inviting you to dinner at our place so that we can all become the close circle that I would like." You're not magically going to create a close, loving circle of best friends here, but you've given it the best diplomatic chance. They may see something you don't, or their opinions may be colored by their own issues about relationships. Whatever the conflict, valid or not, you have taken the situation and given it the best possible chance of resolution.

**Q.** One of my bridesmaids is notoriously late and irresponsible, and it's like pulling teeth to get her to fulfill any of her responsibilities for the wedding. I know she wasn't a good choice to include, but I couldn't leave her out. How can I get her to be more reliable?

**A.** Some people are just chronically late or notoriously flaky. You can't go back in time and not include her in the bridal party, and it's an exercise in futility to expect her to change her personality and the way she's always done things. For your wedding, though, you do expect her to fulfill responsibilities, so create a diplomatic new way of placing a task in front of her.

"[Her name], all of the bridesmaids have sent in their deposits for the gowns, and we're waiting for yours. I don't want to wait any longer than Friday to put the order in, so what's going to work best for you to get me your deposit? I'll be happy to meet you for lunch on Thursday and get your check from you." Some people do need a reward to complete a task that others do willingly out of the goodness of their hearts, so just accept this as the potential solution to the problem. A six-dollar sandwich for her is worth eliminating the headaches of waiting for her to even find her checkbook, let alone write and mail you a check. So this new method may be your best answer. Nagging won't help, and it's not good diplomacy. Setting up these face-to-face meetings, if possible, could be the perfect solution.

If you can't get to her for these solutions, then you'll have to deliver a diplomacy speech that can be among the more difficult to deliver. "[Her name], it's causing me a lot of stress to have to keep calling you to get deposit checks and to have you not show up for dress shopping trips. Is this wedding too much for you right now? We can talk about your stepping out of the wedding, if that works best for you. I'd be disappointed, but I'm wondering if your stalling means you don't really want to be involved. Let's come up with a solution so that we don't have an ongoing problem." You've told her how serious this is for you—she may not have been aware—and offered to help solve the problem. That's way better friend diplomacy than she has shown to you, but you're on the high road, a bride with wonderful perspective and self-value.

**Q.** My maid of honor has turned into the etiquette police, telling me that I can't do certain things the way I'd like to, and—even worse—she's getting the other bridesmaids and my mother to question my every move. She says she just doesn't want me to make any mistakes or embarrass myself, but it's getting really annoying. She did save me from one huge mistake, and she throws that in my face all the time.

**A.**     As much as this maid of honor is doing wrong—especially by running to others with judgments about your every move—there's one little piece of information in here that does matter: She's looking out for you. Maybe there are huge, glaring etiquette rules that you're breaking, and she fears that you'll offend many of your guests and hurt your relationships with them. For instance, a bridesmaid once had to approach the bride about the bride's plan to leave all of her destination wedding guests on their own for meals and activities while the bride planned the last-minute wedding details. Having attended destination weddings in the past, this bridesmaid knew that guests who traveled so far to attend the wedding, and spent so much to be there, would be highly offended if they were left without any kind of cocktail party or luncheon. The bride had, after all, written on the invitation that "We'll take great care of you," and the bridesmaid knew there was no plan for that. The bridesmaid took the risk to say something, and even though the bride didn't appreciate her input at first, the outcome was excellent—all the guests were treated to a cocktail party and a boating trip to go snorkeling. The destination wedding would have been a disaster without the bridesmaid's advice and the bride's follow-through. Your maid of honor doesn't want you in the center of a firestorm.

That said, when the input is to protect you, you are wise to look for the positive in the input. But when the input is more of a bossy nature, nitpicky and judgmental, and based on old-world etiquette of a formality that doesn't match your style, then your diplomatic response is: "[Her name], I appreciate all that you're doing to help me, especially lending your opinions regarding etiquette. But we're planning a very personalized wedding, and we've read in very good wedding books that there are some etiquette rules than can be bent a little bit to allow for personalization. We're being really careful not to offend anyone, so you don't need to keep warning me about potential mistakes, or talking to the other bridesmaids or our mothers about which mistakes you think we're making." Mentioning the specific people she's gone to is far better than saying "other people," since it shows her that you're aware of her gossiping. "We're on top of it, and our wedding coordinator is on top of it as well. So thank you for looking out for me, and don't worry about the etiquette angle anymore. Let's talk about the plans for the after-party instead."

You just provided multiple reasons why you're confident in your plans without resorting to whining that it's your wedding and you'll do things the way you'd like. You've thanked her for her advice—without going near the one time she saved you—and very gently asked her to focus on something else with you. Well done.

**Q.** Some of my bridesmaids are well-off financially, but others are struggling. This is causing a lot of friction when it comes to the gown choices, shoe choices, and the shower. My rich friends want to wear designer gowns, and my less-rich friends are complaining. How can I get them to put their financial standing aside and just be my friends?

**A.** This is a tough one, since different people have different ideas about money. Some friends might find a $300 shoe a bargain, while others have never bought a pair of shoes for more than $29. So make your choices in a style that gives them selections in any price range. For instance, you might say, "I'd like you all to wear little, black cocktail-length dresses—you choice of style, but it has to be black." Your rich friends can go designer while your budget-conscious friends can wear that beautiful little black dress they already own, or find something in their price range.

If you'd like your bridesmaids in a shade of color besides black, then show them a Web site where they can choose their own style of dress. Here's your script for the very wise decision to give your maids some input on the color they'll wear:

"I'd love your input on which color you'll wear. We like the sky blue and the navy blue shown in this link, so if you have any strong opinions on these colors, I'd love to have your 'vote' by Tuesday."

You've given them a voice in the matter, but it's clear that you'll be making the decision and setting the deadline. If anyone writes back about a third choice of color, here's your line: "It is pretty, isn't it? I looked at that color and it doesn't work for our wedding theme. We're keeping it to the sky blue and navy blue, so which one do you prefer?"

Done! You've politely eliminated the confusion of the third color choice, and you've smoothly kept the options to your own two choices.

For shoes, "wear your own" black, strappy heels allows them to choose the designer and price point. The ladies will love to make their own choices.

As for the shower, talk to the maid of honor or person in charge. "First of all, thank you for taking on the shower. I have one request, though. I don't want some of my friends who are in law school right now with huge student loans to be financially pressed, so please keep that in mind as a favor to me. If this were your bridal shower, I'd be in the circle of people who need a budget break, so please keep things on the less expensive side. Thank you." How do you offer ideas on how this can be done without being a control freak? Here's your script: "Here's an idea that worked really well at my cousin's wedding: Instead of everyone splitting a percentage of the party, ask them which tasks they want to handle, and let them do it according to their budget levels. Marci can do the invitations for free, for instance. She has great invitation software that I love, and it would be great to let her make the invitations and place cards as her contribution. Tania can make the favors, since she is starting up her own line of aromatherapy soaps and lotions." Your maid of honor and the richer bridesmaids might not have known the wealth and value in your lower-budget friends' potential contributions.

Secure your bridal party's budget with the following: "These women are all important friends of mine, and they're all in places in their lives where they're investing their money in their educations, careers, and new homes. When I asked them to be in the bridal party, I promised them that the financial expense wouldn't be high, so I'm asking you to honor my promise to them." That should do it, providing your maid of honor is a decent friend or sister who would do anything to please you.

If you still see class warfare going on, that's just bad character on their parts, and you may have to step in with a harsher warning to the maid of honor. "I'd like the clashes between you all to stop. If you can't work together with decency, then I won't have you working together at all. I'll hand the shower over to another friend, and then none of you will have to deal with each other. I'm so disappointed to hear any of my friends either upset or bragging about making someone else upset, so I'm prepared to take some steps here to solve the problem. You're my maid of honor, and I'm counting on you to set some new ground rules. I'll be happy to talk it over with you if you'd like any ideas, but I know you can handle this."

As for the battling bridesmaids, send them all an e-mail with your request. "I'd like you all to call a truce and stop the complaining about each other. You're all very important to me, so please just try to get along with one another." No need to go into how they're ruining the wedding for you. Keep it short and to the point.

**Q.** Two of my bridesmaids are mad that they weren't chosen as maid of honor. They quoted a wedding book to me, which said that brides can choose more than one, and they want to know why I chose our one friend over them.

**A.** "Because the person I chose would never try to manipulate me into a choice by shaking a wedding book at me," is the answer I'm sure we all wish we could deliver and call it a day, but for the sake of keeping your character and relationships intact, you'll need to elevate your approach to a better form of diplomacy. Your diplomatic answer is based in honesty. "I'm a traditionalist, and I wanted only one maid of honor. [Your choice] has been a friend of mine since the second grade, and while I love you all equally, the long amount of time I spent thinking about this led to a decision that I feel very comfortable with. I'm sorry that you're offended, but this is the choice that I wanted to make. I'm thrilled to have you both as my bridesmaids, and I see my entire bridal party as equals. So please don't take it personally, since this has nothing to do with how I feel about you." You'll deliver this, of course, with love and understanding for them, not with any venomous comparisons about how this friend of yours would never try to guilt you into naming her as maid of honor, or that their attitude with you has convinced you that you made the right choice. That may be true—it probably is—but it's not going to work toward any harmony or diplomacy for your group's future working conditions. It's purely bad form for any bridesmaid to try to weasel her way into a higher "rank," and your diplomatic, reasonable answer is perhaps more respectful than they deserve.

**Q.** My friends are leaving my sister out of the planning. My sister is older, and they're being very rude to her.

**A.** An older, more mature bridesmaid is going to be perplexed by the "mean girls" clique's methods that target her and—in the minds of her taunting, teasing, excluding cohorts in the bridal party—cast her aside. Psychologists say that group dynamics lower the IQ of the people in the group to the lowest common denominator (i.e., the biggest loser in the group), and when cliques form against a decent and upstanding person, making her an outsider, this becomes a repeat of the fifth-grade playground, which is not an acceptable condition for your bridal party. The mean girls require a talking to, and your firm request is an investment in the happiness of your sister as well as your relationships with all of these women. So approach the clique and say, "I've noticed that you're having a lot of planning sessions for the wedding and completely leaving my sister out." Don't say that your sister is hurt by their actions, as that is their payoff; It's exactly why they do it. "I find that offensive, and I'm asking you now to stop with the division and honor my request to make you all equal bridesmaids. If there's something you need to gather to do, send my sister an e-mail or give her a call. When she has an opinion, I'd like you to respect her the way you'd respect me. I'm sure this wasn't intentional, but I don't like what I'm seeing, and I know that you're all decent enough to change the way you're operating."

You'll say this calmly, of course, but directly. The mean girls in your bridal party will be stunned to be spoken to with such authority, and, if they're worthy of your company, they'll treat your sister with more respect and kindness. If they still mistreat your sister, fire them from the bridal party. Anyone who hurts your family member is not truly a friend at all. This kind of behavior has no place in a bridal party, since this is a position of honor given to those you trust, depend on, and love. These girls' characters are in question as things stand now, but you might just find that they weren't intentionally being mean or exclusive. They may not have been aware that your older sister would want to meet up with them for drinks and wedding talk. Hand over her e-mail address or cell number—with her permission, of course—and make it easier for them to treat your sister as they would treat you. Friends come and go, but sisters last forever.

**Q.** My bridesmaids can't come to a decision on anything. Not the dresses, the shoes, the shower— nothing. Can I take over the decisions for them, just to get things done? I wouldn't want to be told what to do, but they're driving me insane.

**A.** Take the middle ground. You're not taking over, you're just limiting their choices . . . while still leaving decisions to them. Since this is a group that can't compromise or agree on anything when given the entire world of fashion and shower dates to choose from, send them an e-mail with a statement of: "I understand you're finding way too many terrific options, and that deciding on one is a challenge. I'm going to make it easier on you all, since I don't want anyone getting overwhelmed or annoyed. Here are the three dresses I've chosen for you all to agree on, and here's the best part—they all come in coordinating colors, so you don't have to agree on one style. As long as you're in this designer's iceberg blue color, any of these styles would work. As for the shoes, they don't have to match identically. I'd like you all to wear silver, strappy heels." Don't go too far by giving them dates for the shower, or places. Just go on faith that once you've relieved them of too many choices with the dresses and the shoes, they can focus on the shower on their own. They may just love this system of yours so much that they'll use it to plan the shower. "If you have any questions, just let me know. I'm happy to help in any way possible to make this an enjoyable experience for you all," is the perfect diplomatic closer.

**Q.** My bridesmaids have been making a lot of suggestions to help with the wedding, and while I appreciated it at first, it's really stressing me out. I'm overwhelmed with everyone's input and want them to just shut up about the wedding right now. How can I tell them to keep their suggestions to themselves?

**A.** Just send them an e-mail: "I love it that you're all so excited about the wedding, and that you're taking the time to send me all these links and ideas. However, I'm starting to feel really overwhelmed with so many opinions (the moms are sending me twice as many e-mails as all of you put together!). So let's save the idea sessions for a girls' night out sometime soon. Don't get me wrong—I do appreciate your enthusiasm. I just don't want to get stressed out from too much of a good thing and turn into one of those horrible bridezillas like on TV. Thanks for understanding. Love, [your name]." You've stated your request and explained why, told them they're not doing anything wrong, and made a plan for a get-together, which is always a great diplomatic approach to dealing with all of your bridesmaids.

**Q.** I hear from my bridesmaids that my maid of honor is being really bossy with them. Since it's their word only, and it doesn't sound like my maid of honor's personality, what's the best way to ask her about this without her getting mad at them?

**A.** Everyone has their own interpretation of other people's personalities, so that may be at the core of this problem. Perhaps the bridesmaids just don't like dealing with an assertive leader, or they're not prepared to handle the responsibilities of being a bridesmaid. In that case, any instructions might come across as bossy. Or, it may be true that the power has gone to your maid of honor's head, and she really is being bossy. Since you're wise to admit that this is a their-word-only situation, you know that your diplomacy position is one of tact. You'll need to approach both sides with a message to "just get along." Start with your maid of honor, and say:

**YOU:** "I'm feeling like the bridesmaids aren't taking to being team players. How are you feeling about working with them?"

**MAID OF HONOR:** "Everything is fine!" She may say this just to spare your feelings and limit the drama.

**YOU:** "No, I'm not sensing that everything is fine," is your response. "I'm seeing that the bridesmaids are not as much of a cohesive group as I'd like them to be." You're not saying that the bridesmaids complained to you, since that will only put the maid of honor on the defensive and could perhaps fuel the fire of conflict between them all.

**MAID OF HONOR:** "I can't get them to agree on a shower date," or some other detail like that.

Here's where you give the maid of honor your perspective with your friends and sisters; try saying: "I've found from planning vacations with them that they don't like being told what to do, and they can be a little oversensitive about it. What works for me is giving them three dates to choose from, just to make it easier." Use what you know. With the other bridesmaids, ask in the same direct manner.

**YOU:** "I'm not sensing that you're enjoying working with my sister. I'd love for you all to get along and work well together, so what can I do to help you all out? What is it about her style that's bugging you? What is she doing that comes off as bossy?"

**BRIDESMAIDS:** "She e-mails every week!" or "She asks us to send a check and then she calls two days later to see if we sent it." It might be a familiar message to you. You love your sister, but you know she can be a little bit intense and super-organized.

**YOU:** "Ah, yes, I know she can be very structured, but she has good intentions, she wants to do a good job, and she wants the shower to be perfect. So can you just work together as best you can, see it as her being overly efficient for my sake, and as long as she's not being mean or rude to you, just peacefully coexist for just a few more months? Again, I really would like for you to all get along and work well together."

That should do it. You're not asking anyone to change . . . you're smoothing the lines between how one performs and how the others can adapt to keep their eyes on the success of the wedding.

**Q.** Two of my bridesmaids are arguing about the shower plans. Since I'm not the host, I don't have much say in what they do. But how can I step in and

**get them to at least be respectful of each other? As of now, they want to do separate showers, which would over-obligate the other bridesmaids.**

**A.** Diplomacy often means mediation between two people who have different styles, who clash with each other, or who have power issues. Not everyone fits together into a working partnership, and not everyone can see their own situation objectively enough to create a good give-and-take. They're too focused on "winning," which is a deeper issue that one or both may have. It has nothing to do with your shower. It's just the way they're wired. That's where you come in. Even though you're not the host of the shower, these two women are close to you, and their struggle upsets you. So talk to both of them separately and let them know you're uncomfortable with how they're clashing. Show your friend acceptance and appreciation for being involved with the shower, and tell her what you love about her planning style and ideas.

Try saying: "Understand that [other bridesmaid] is just different than you, and she has a very different working style than you have. So let's find a way to make some changes to your partnership on this shower without asking either of you to change who you are."

That's often enough to get them listening. You're not going to tell her to defer to the bossier bridesmaid, and you're not going to tell her to lighten up. "Now what can I do to help you both co-create this shower? If you had two close friends in this situation, what would you do?"

Now you've given her a different perspective. Often, people reveal the very solution they're seeking when they're "talking about someone else."

Even though it's not your gathering to plan, you might decide to divide up their tasks so that they're each working with other bridesmaids on the menu, the favors, and so on. Ask them for the tasks they'd like to work on, and where they both claim the same task (like the flowers), you "divide the baby" by breaking down that one big task into two smaller tasks. One gets the floral centerpieces, and the other gets the décor.

Now, don't appoint a "boss" for them. They may not be able to work together, but if you say, "You'll both be working with my mother now, and she'll be making the big decisions," that's a powder keg. It seems like it would be a good idea, but the friends can get insulted. After all, they are devoting their time and finances to your party. They just can't get along due to personality differences that are never going to change. Demoting them and having them answer to a third person is not the best tactic. It might turn into a last resort, but it's not your first diplomatic approach.

If they're still clashing, even though you're trying an approach that they helped create, the problem goes way deeper. It might be a good idea to allow them to plan separate bridal showers after all, if that seems like the best alternative or if they belong to separate circles of friends and family. A bride can have several showers for this very reason. So don't count it out if your bridesmaids request having separate events for you. Just reply with: "Yes, that sounds like a great idea. Thank you." There's no need to go into how you were thinking about the same solution, or how it will save them trouble, and so on. Just be a gracious receiver.

## Keeping the Peace

Sometimes your first attempt won't be completely effective. You may have to try several times to get the right solution.

**Q.** A few of my bridesmaids don't seem to care about the wedding plans. They say it's too early to do all the planning. It's hurting me that they're not sharing in my happiness, so how can I tell them that now is when I'm planning, and there won't be tasks to do later?

**A.** That's exactly what you tell them. Whether or not they've ever planned a wedding, some people act according to what they think the process should be like. Your bridesmaids believe their roles start months down the road. But as the bride, you're telling them the clock starts now. I'd suggest talking to each of them, not sending an e-mail, so that they can hear in your voice that you're excited about your wedding plans and excited to include them. Just say: "Since my schedule is going to be very packed months down the road,

I'm handling all of my wedding plans now. I'm really excited about the dress shopping trip for your gowns, so which Sundays do you have open in the next three weeks?" Keep it to a specific thing, not a vague "I want you to be involved." You've just presented an actual plan to them while at the same time being respectful of their schedules. If anyone says, "It's too early," your diplomatic answer is: "Not for me, it's not. Which Sundays do you have open?"

**Q.** I don't have room to give my bridesmaids an "and guest" for wedding dates. None of my single friends will get an "and guest," and my bridesmaids are angry that they're not getting special consideration because they're in the bridal party.

**A.** This one makes a lot of people angry. In old-world etiquette, every adult over the age of eighteen gets an "and guest," but some brides and grooms need to chop those extra spaces out to make room for their closest friends and family. Since you've made this decision not to give out "and guests" to single friends, just tell the bridal party the following:

"While we wish we could give you special consideration due to your stature in the wedding, it's just not possible. As of the current guest headcount, we're in the unenviable position of having to leave many of our friends, family, neighbors, and coworkers off the wedding list. It wasn't an easy decision, and we don't like how unhappy everyone is about it, but I'm asking for your understanding since we have to stand by our decision. We wish it could be different, and this really stinks, but it's what we have to do."

**Q.** I told my bridesmaids that they could choose their own styles of gowns in the same color, and they ordered their choices. I've since found out that two of them chose super-sexy styles that won't be appropriate at our wedding. Can I ask them to order something different?

**A.** As the bride, you can ask your bridesmaids to choose more appropriate dresses. If it's a case where your church doesn't allow bare shoulders or plunging necklines, you'll send an e-mail or make a call: "Hi [bridesmaid]. Thanks for sending me the link to your choice of dress for the wedding. There is a problem, though. Our church doesn't allow bare shoulders, and I'm sorry I didn't think to tell you that ahead of time. So if you'll do me the favor of picking another style of dress that covers your shoulders, I'll pay for the shipping on your return for that strapless dress. Sorry for the inconvenience, and thanks for understanding."

Most dresses can be returned if the bridesmaids bought them from a department store. But if it was at a bridal shop, returns will likely not be possible. Here's your solution:

Say: "Since I know that you can't return the dress, here's a link to some very pretty jackets that would work well with your dress style. I read that a lot of brides and bridesmaids who want to go strapless wear a jacket or wrap during the ceremony, and I like that solution for you and for any other bridesmaids who chose the strapless gown."

Should you offer to pay for the jacket? No, you don't have to say anything about that unless you green-lighted the sexy, strapless dress in the first place. If a bridesmaid ordered a dress without first checking with you—which is bad form—she foots the bill for the necessary cover-up. Here's your script:

**BRIDESMAID:** "You're paying for this new jacket, right?"

**YOU:** "No, the jacket counts as part of your wedding wardrobe, and since I'm not helping any of the brides-maids with their gowns, that would open a can of worms if they found out that I bought part of your ensemble."

**BRIDESMAID:** "But I paid $150 for the dress, and now I have to pay more? For a jacket that *you* suggested? Because you want me to cover up?"

There's no need to launch into how upset you are that she chose a super-sexy dress style. Stay away from any form of judgment and smooth this brewing conflict over with:

**YOU:** "You know I've always admired your sense of adventure when it comes to your personal style because I'm so much more traditional, but I'm afraid your choice of dress might offend some of my family who still see weddings as old-world affairs. If I agree to pay for ship-ping and handling, would you consider another dress?"

You're focused on the solution without insulting your bridesmaid's taste.

**Q.** One of my bridesmaids is going to be very pregnant on our wedding day, and we're concerned about her because it's going to be an outdoor wedding, in the summer, at an island destination. She's been told by her doctor not to fly in her third trimester. She's not respecting her doctor's advice, so should we fire her from the bridal party?

**A.** No friend would allow another friend to put her baby in danger three different ways. Some people take unwise risks because they want to be included, or they think they're indestructible, but this is not a situation where anyone should gamble. Just tell her, "I'm very uncomfortable about you flying to our wedding when the doctor said you shouldn't, and the fact that it's going to be hot outside also makes me worry. I'd never be able to forgive myself if something happened to your baby, or to you, so I'm going to have to do the right thing and ask you to step out of the bridal party." Not "remove you from the bridal party." "We're having a big celebration when we get back, and given this situation, I'm going to do a big presentation on my honor attendants at that party, so would you please be in my bridal party for that celebration? Again, I love you and want you in my lineup, but I can't risk your safety or the baby's with that destination wedding." If you've lost sleep on this one, tell her so. Tell her you don't want to hurt her feelings. But don't go anywhere near anything that sounds like, "you're not taking this seriously, but I am." Stick with just your wedding, not your deeper concerns that she's not being protective enough of her pregnancy. That's not your problem to solve.

**Q.** Several of my friends are getting married close to the same time as my wedding. Can I ask them to leave the dates of my showers and rehearsal alone so that I can have those days?

**A.** Yes, you absolutely can—if you're firm on the dates for all of those celebrations. It wouldn't be fair for you to block off multiple dates. It's good diplomacy to handle this "marking of your days" with humor, and with your sparkling personality. Send a quick e-mail reading, "Hey girls, we just wanted to let you know that our dates have been set for the showers and rehearsal, and since it wouldn't be much fun without you, we thought we'd give you plenty of advance notice as a save the date." You've achieved the objective, and shown your value in the friendships. Don't be surprised if you get similar save the dates back from them as they admire and emulate your idea. You're not asking, you're expressing your plans with an inclusive tone, and giving them VIP treatment when they hear before anyone else. No need to mention anything else in this note along with the dates, times, and places of the events. If you go too far and—even jokingly—say that you've beaten them to the best days, your diplomacy backfires.

**Q.** A few of my bridesmaids are big partiers and, frankly, they don't act like ladies when they're drinking. How can I tell them to behave themselves around my family and friends?

**A.** This is another tough one, since your friends will likely not enjoy being judged by you—especially if you've had regular wild nights out with the girls. And if you haven't shared their partying lifestyle, your request could hit a nerve with them. If anyone else has ever told them to ease up on the drinking and club lifestyle, your innocent request to tone it down takes on a much greater weight than you may realize. So you'll have to be very diplomatic at how you phrase your request:

"We're saving the harder partying for the after-party, girls, since I'll need you all to be semi-sober in case there's anything to be done during the reception. We're going to be taking lots of pictures, and we'll have special dances throughout the night. My relatives are very conservative, and I don't mean to be offensive in any way, but I'm asking the *entire* bridal party to keep it at half-throttle until we get to the full-throttle after-parties. I really want to enjoy the reception with all of you, and not have anyone miss out on anything."

You haven't been judgmental, although they will read that in what you said. The fact is, you can't control how people will act on their own, but you've given it a good diplomatic effort and stated your request for what you'd like for your reception. If they get offended, which might happen, know that it could be the hold that alcohol has on their lives that keeps them from acting rationally and considerately toward you. They also might be a bit immature, so they might not take this request as well as a more even-keeled bridesmaid. Just do your best with this one, and hope for the best.

Some people can't control themselves if there is alcohol in the room, and their behavior is only a reflection on them. If they act like fools at the reception, ask the site manager to approach them with a request to get down off the table, or put them in a cab. Wait until after your glorious honeymoon to assess the friendship's value to your future.

**Q.** One of my bridesmaids has a very big tattoo on her back, and the gown choice will show it. I'd like to suggest a tattoo cover-up cream, but I'm afraid she's going to be upset with me. It's a memorial tattoo for a departed relative of hers, but it's really big and really inappropriate.

**A.** If you ask her to cover up a tattoo that means a lot to her, then she's going to be the one who needs to remove her emotion and find a calm diplomacy to handle you. Your bridesmaids are in your lineup because you love them. Brides who get too wrapped up in making sure their bridesmaids all conform to their image of perfection with matching hairstyles, matching jewelry, and matching lipstick are actually treating their best friends and sisters like accessories. Imagine if you had a scar on your shoulder or a tattoo, and a bride told you to "cover that thing up with this" as she slapped a cover cream in your hand. Wouldn't you be embarrassed and a little bit angry? Wouldn't you think, "Who is she to tell me to cover up a scar or tattoo?" and "Why is this a big deal now when she previously told me she loved the tattoo?" I'd advise skipping this request, since some cover creams do work well at first and then fade or run as the bridesmaid gets sweaty on the dance floor. Anyway, everyone will be looking at you.

**Q.** My bridesmaids keep hitting on my fiancé's brother, who, admittedly, is very hot. The girls are acting very juvenile and aggressive, and it's upsetting both my fiancé and his brother. How can I tell my girls to cool it?

**A.** The most diplomatic approach to this all-too-common problem when some bridesmaids never got the memo to act like ladies is to be direct. "Look, you are falling all over yourselves and making fools of yourselves by hitting on [fiancé's brother]. He has a girlfriend, and they, [fiancé], and their family are all getting really uncomfortable with the way you're acting. So please stop with the flirting, okay?"

You haven't called them any names, and you haven't compared their behavior to anything on a seedy daytime talk show, but you got the message across that people they should be respecting right now are not pleased with their behavior and would like them to stop.

**Q.** One of my bridesmaids is crying poverty, and asking me to pay for her gown, when I know she just booked a vacation to Europe with her friends. How can I say no to her request?

**A.** Some people are very good at conning their way through life. They see it as a game that they're very good at, beating the system and winning over others who are going by the rules. This bridesmaid has some nerve to be so grabby while she's bragging about her European vacation. It's not the smartest diplomacy to mention her exorbitant trip, since that makes you sound like you measure as well. Just say, "No, I'm sorry, but I'm not going to be able to help you out financially. I am doing everything I can to get you a lower-priced dress and shoes, and I'm working to keep your expenses under $300." You've just told her that she's already benefiting from your efforts, and you didn't step into any murky waters that give a manipulator something to work with.

What about reminding her that she agreed to be in the bridal party knowing that the role would entail some expense? A gentle reminder is in order here, not a scolding. Here's what you say: "I know the expense of being in a bridal party can sometimes add up to a lot, but we're all working really hard to keep everyone's expenses low." Don't say, "Back when I asked you to be in the bridal party, I did say that you'd be responsible for your gown, shoes, and travel to the wedding, and you said that wasn't a problem." That will only open up a rebuttal such as, "Well, I didn't know how much it would be!" delivered with a big whine. That's not going to get you to a solution; stick with your firmly delivered no.

**Q.** I'd like to help one of my bridesmaids with her expenses, but not let the others know. What do I say if they do find out?

**A.** If they do find out, your diplomacy goes right for their empathy. "[Bridesmaid] is having a little bit of hardship right now, and I offered to help her out, since she's helped me out in the past." That's it. Don't invite disaster by trying to make extra excuses or explaining why you didn't offer financial help to anyone else. Often, in your attempts to preempt a problem, you create one. Just leave the topic there, and move on. If someone calls and asks for a matching "donation," just tell the truth. Your wedding budget is bursting at the seams, and you're not able to help everyone out in the same way. You handled that problem when it came up, as a personal matter between the two of you. (No need to get into the "who told you?" thing, because secrets do come out—sometimes innocently—and it doesn't matter who blabbed about this one.) Here's what you say: "I wish I could help you, but I'm doing all I can to save all of my bridesmaids money on everything from the dresses to their lodgings. That's the best I can do, and I hope you understand."

**Q.** My bridesmaids are planning something really inappropriate for my bridal shower. I said no to a male exotic dancer for my bachelorette party—we're going to a spa instead—and I found out they've booked the dancer for my shower. My grandmothers will be there. The bridesmaid who told me doesn't want me to yell at them, but I have to get them to cancel.

**A.** This one takes a stricter form of diplomacy. This is something you absolutely do not want, so make the calls to the bridesmaids, and use this script:

**YOU:** "I've heard that you booked a male dancer for my shower, which is really inappropriate considering my grandmothers will be there, as will my flower girls and nieces. I said no to it for my bachelorette party for a reason—it's not my style, it's not what I want, and I promised my fiancé that there would not be one. Period."

## Keeping the Peace

As a matter of good wedding diplomacy, when you're requiring so much of your family and friends, it's best if you take on the legwork and do all you can—rather than delegate—to help them out.

**BRIDESMAID:** "Oh, lighten up! Your shower is supposed to be fun! And don't you think the guys are going to have strippers at their party?"

**YOU:** "No, actually, I don't, because my fiancé promised me that he'd refuse his groomsmen's plans for that as well. So please cancel it right now, or you're going to lose a lot of your money when I have the guy thrown out if he shows up at my party." Use a firm and assertive voice, letting them know that this is not up for discussion.

**BRIDESMAID:** "Well, what if we just got a male dancer for the later hours of the party when your grandmothers aren't there?"

She's assuming that's your problem. She's trying anything to get her way. Just say: "My answer is no. Please cancel it now."

**Q.** My bridesmaids want to stay at my house on the wedding weekend, to save money on hotel bills after all they've spent on the wedding. It would be chaos, and I can't afford to pay for their hotel rooms. How can I tell them to find someone else to crash with?

**A.** I know you're thinking about how much they're spending to be in your wedding party, and you don't want them to be upset about your turning down their request. So here's what you say: "I wish I could let you all stay at my place, but it's just not going to work. Things are going to be very hectic then, and I'm going to need a quiet, peaceful place and plenty of room at my house to do all the last-minute things. But let me make some calls to some friends who have guest rooms, and I'll check out some less expensive but nice hotels and bed-and-breakfasts. I'll help you all coordinate your lodging." When you show that you care about their lodging, it means just as much as if you paid for their stays. Suggest that they share a suite, and show them how the prices break down with six to a big room. Never tell them to "just go look online."

**Q.** One of my bridesmaids needs to get out of the bridal party due to personal problems. How can I let others know she's out without having them ask what's going on?

**A.** They're going to be intrigued and concerned, of course—wouldn't you be?—but the best diplomatic answer is, "She and I discussed what's best for her, and this is the decision that we agreed on. She's having a difficult time, but she's going to be fine. This just takes some of the pressure off of her." Of course, it's best if you ask her what she'd like you to say in addition to or instead of that, giving her some control over the situation for herself. Her closest friends will call and support her, with you among them. Don't get lost in your wedding and forget to be there for her.

# Chapter 3

# Groomsmen Grief

Ah, the groomsmen. They're your brothers, your fiancé's best friends, and—love 'em or hate 'em—they're a big part of your wedding picture. Not much has been written about the care and handling of groomsmen, since traditional bridal magazines and Web sites pretty much stick to the basics of getting these guys tuxedoed and accessorized. But these men, facing your dreams of their being courtly gentlemen and very often missing the mark due to various states of arrested development, frat-boy machismo, or simple absenteeism, require an ultra-delicate form of diplomacy. Why so delicate with the men? Because, more often than not, they're your fiancé's friends and brothers. He's fine with their behavior, but you want socially acceptable manners. He doesn't worry what people will think of his friends, but . . . well, you probably do. So this puts you in what could be a very loaded situation. How do you tell his friends and brothers they have to behave themselves without everyone getting mad at you?

Of course, not all groomsmen are Neanderthals or frat-minded. Many are wonderful, thoughtful, considerate, timely, and classy. You won't have a diplomacy problem with those groomsmen, so we'll focus on the troublemakers to arm you with the most diplomatic solutions for the problems they cause.

**Q.** The groomsmen are party boys. I'd like my fiancé to tell them to behave themselves at the wedding, but he's not willing to give them a lecture. Should I?

**A.** Before I get into this one, let me ask you a question. Do you have a friend who's very whiny, self-absorbed, bossy, spoiled, or a party girl who has been known to get sloppy during nights out? Do you love that friend anyway? You're used to her, it's harmless, and she's a great friend who's been there for you in the past. Now, what if your fiancé wanted you to approach that friend and say, "Hey, can you please do your best not to be whiny and self-absorbed on the wedding day, because you might embarrass us?" It's unlikely that you'd jump right up to deliver the lecture. That's the position your fiancé might feel like he's in right now. He knows his guys better than you do, and he trusts they'll have fun at the wedding but that they won't drive a car through the building or bring live goats into the reception. "You're overreacting," your fiancé might say. "They'll be fine." And you're stewing for the rest of the day.

I'm not saying that your concerns aren't valid, or that the men should be left to act like spring breakers at your wedding just because your fiancé doesn't want a confrontation. I'm just reminding you of diplomatic perspective—seeing the first part of the problem from your fiancé's point of view. Of course he's not going to lecture his friends if he doesn't believe they're a threat to the wedding, and it's not a good idea to use this as a test of his love for you ("If you love me, you'll talk to them!" or "I'm not asking for very much, sweetie!"). Yuck. Manipulation doesn't look very good on anyone.

With that said, and once you've decided on just how big a threat their behavior is to your wedding, it's time for you to create your own plan of diplomatic approach. It won't work to e-mail them six months before the wedding to ask them to refrain from drinking too much at the wedding. They'll wave that off and forget all about it. Timing is on your side when you talk to your entire bridal party at the rehearsal dinner. Not at the rehearsal, where you're all focused on much more essential things. The rehearsal itself gets everyone in the mind-set that there is serious work to be done and an amount of decorum and manners that are very important at a wedding ceremony. You'll then build on that mindset when you end the rehearsal itself and set off for the celebration that night. Take your bridal party (minus the little ones) to the side and thank them for their participation in your wedding and their presence in your lives.

Start by saying: "We're very happy to have you all as our inner circle." That's a nice way to put it that reminds them of the honor it is for them to be there with you. "Everything that takes place on the wedding day is a reflection of us, and of our parents, and of all the people we care about, so thanks in advance for being a part of it. And since we will be celebrating with our parents and our extended families, and our bosses and colleagues, we'd like you to stay semi-sober and save the hard partying for the after-party, okay?" You've made your expectations clear, rather than expecting anyone in your group to mind-read your wishes for decorum. There's no need to single out the worst offender, as in, "John, try not to get drunk and hit on my mother." You don't want to insult your group, or act like a scolding parent.

## Keeping the Peace

When it comes to wrangling drunk guests, let the site staff step in for you. They're not worried about diplomacy or future relationships, so they can be far more assertive in motivating the inebriated offender to have a cup of coffee or get in a cab.

If someone gets too intoxicated at the wedding, you will have someone nearby who can remove that person. Your presence in your wedding outfits carries a lot of authority on the wedding day, so, in the moment, if a groomsman is stumbling and slurring, you both can certainly take him aside and ask him to slow down. If you don't want to approach him on your wedding day, a wedding coordinator or site manager knows just how to remove a drunk person, and they won't worry about hurting his feelings.

**Q.** The groomsmen are way, way late with sending in their size cards and payment for the tuxes. They have nearly no responsibilities, and they can't even get this right. I'm ready to start calling them daily to get them to move on it.

**A.** Whether it's your slow groomsmen or your glacially slow bridesmaids, repeated nagging isn't going to work. What will work is spelling out the effects of the delay very diplomatically. Your fiancé can take on this task, or delegate it to his best man.

For example, your fiancé or his best man can say: "[Groomsman], we're looking at a deadline of March 5 to get the size cards in. Anything after that puts us all into the time window for a rush order, which is going to cost you $50 more. Not only that, but the order for all the guys' tuxes has to go in together, so if you're late, everyone's order will be late, and then they will have to pay the extra $50, too. So we'd really like for you to get the size card to us by Thursday."

The guy might not mean to be late with the size card; he might just not know what to do. Your fiancé can offer assistance in helping him find a tailor who can take his measurements, and if you both feel the groomsmen need extra incentive to get the size cards together, perhaps your fiancé can offer to take them all to lunch after a group size-taking at the tailor's or tux shop. That kind of outing can be planned with just a few days' notice when the guys are slow in getting this task done on their own. Your fiancé can e-mail them all with the plan and invitation.

When they do send in their size cards, you and your fiancé should send them a quick e-mail with your thanks. Positive reinforcement now helps with future tasks and diplomacy needs.

**Q.** My fiancé promised that he'd pay for his guys' hotel rooms, but we don't have room in our budget for that. We'd have to cut out something I like. Is it possible to take back the offer? He really wasn't thinking.

**A.** The diplomacy of this problem is in your fiancé's court. He made the offer, but you don't know if the groomsmen initially said it wasn't necessary before acquiescing so as not to be rude. Since these are the closest men in his life, all he has to do is call or e-mail them with this wording: "The wedding budget's grown a bit, and while I know I offered to pay for your rooms, I didn't factor it into the budget. If any of you are willing to forego the free room, I'd be grateful." It's important that he phrase it this way, instead of in a perceived "safe" way—such as blaming you. The groomsmen who initially said "not necessary" to the free room offer will likely be fine with paying for their own, although some might not give up their freebie due to their own financial limits. If they weren't expecting to pay for the room, they didn't budget for it. Ask your fiancé to do all he can to get the guys well-priced hotel rooms, or check out suites that four of them can share with their dates for much less per couple or per person. If you both can arrange for the guys to stay with friends of theirs in the area, that's a fine solution.

**Q.** My fiancé wants one of his friends to be a groomsman, but he's recently divorced from one of my bridesmaids, and they hate each other. They met through us, and he's not an absolute best friend of my fiancé, whereas my bridesmaid is one of my best friends. Can I tell him to make another choice?

**A.** In theory, your fiancé is free to ask anyone he wants to be a part of the bridal party, but when reality enters the picture, a good conversation between you could show that a different choice might indeed be better.

Start by saying: "I'm concerned that the tension between [groomsman] and [bridesmaid] will really put a damper on our ceremony. They absolutely hate each other, and I don't want to be taking our vows in the middle of their stare-down. I know you're not absolute best friends with [groomsman], so would you please consider leaving him out of the bridal party?" If your fiancé has already asked him, then you'll have to hope for maturity and respect from your friends. Here is what you can say to the two of them: "We know that the two of you have a difficult history and that there's still a lot of tension between you, but we both want the two of you in our bridal party. Is there anything we can do to make this more comfortable for you?" You're not saying, "behave yourselves," but you're getting that point across. By phrasing it as a question, you allow them to assure you that they will coexist in peace.

If your fiancé can boot his friend from the party, but is concerned about not having another man to fill the space, assure him that bridal parties don't have to be equal numbers of men and women. He doesn't need to fill the spot.

**Q.** The guys want to wear a really inexpensive style of tuxedo to keep their costs down, and they also think it would be "fun" to wear ruffled shirts. Where did they get the idea that it's their choice? How can I get them to wear what I've chosen for them?

**A.** As a gracious bride and groom, you can choose their style of wardrobe, nix the ruffled shirts, and assure them that you have their budgets in mind. Don't start off the conversation by saying "Where did you get the idea that it's your choice?" That shuts down negotiations in a flash, and lowers their opinion of you. It's pretty rare that groomsmen would be emotionally invested in what they're wearing to a wedding, so consider the possibility that they're just kidding—and successfully teasing you. Most do care about how they're going to look, but they know they take their instructions from you. So present several possibilities to them, either in person or via links in an e-mail. You and your fiancé can say to them: "Hello guys! We've spent some time looking for great tuxes for you, and here are our top contenders. Just let us know by Friday which you prefer most, and we'll choose the one that gets the most votes." You've just performed excellent diplomacy with the men. You kept the message short and to the point, given them a limited number of choices, and set a deadline for them to respond. And just forget about the ruffled shirt idea, because they've probably forgotten about it by now. If they ask about it, just smile and say, "We've decided to go in a different direction."

**Q.** The guys are being really insensitive about dancing with some of the bridesmaids. They've made up horrible nicknames for my friends and are being extremely rude.

**A.** No doubt your friends wouldn't want to socialize with classless creatures such as these, so don't require them to dance together at the reception. Your friends can dance with their dates, and these guys can drag their knuckles around the room hoping to meet someone they can entertain for the evening. If anything disparaging is said about your friends in your presence, feel free to reproach the guys with a simple, "Please don't talk about my friends like that."

**Q.** I've heard the guys are planning a raunchy bachelor's party for my fiancé, and I really don't want that to happen. We are fighting about it, because he doesn't want to look wimpy by telling them I'm against it.

**A.** The current remedy for the unwanted raunchy bachelor's party is to plan a shared, coed bachelor/bachelorette party, where the group goes out together to dinner, a sporting event, or even a weekend trip to Las Vegas or the beach. As the bride and groom, you can contact your maid of honor and best man with the following script: "We'd like you to know that rather than separate bachelor and bachelorette parties, we'd like to plan a coed party or a trip to Vegas, or maybe go see a basketball game all together. We'd love for all of our friends to be together for one big shared party." Plenty of brides and grooms are taking the party out of their honor attendants' hands and planning their own coed party as a way to control the raunch factor and save their friends the budget-crunch of paying for a larger party than they expected.

Here's your script if you like that plan: "We're going to host our own coed bachelor/bachelorette party at [location] on [date]. We'll be sending out invitations to everyone in a few weeks, but we just wanted you to know that you won't have to plan anything. We've got it all taken care of."

Now if your fiancé *wants* the bachelor party with his friends, there's not much you can do about it other than ask your fiancé and the trusted men who will be in attendance to keep your relationship in mind at the party. Here's what you say: "I'm not happy about this party, but I know you want to have a good time with your friends. If I tell them, 'no strippers,' I know they're going to get strippers anyway. My brother is going to be there, as is my brother-in-law, and so many of our friends, so please don't make a fool of yourself or of me. That's not a good way to start off our life together. I promise that I'll honor our relationship at the bachelorette's party."

## Keeping the Peace

After the bachelor/bachelorette party, you'll both have to decide on what you prefer—full disclosure about what went on at the celebration, or not to talk about it. Some people feel the full disclosure thing is much like being interrogated, while others know that it would be better for them to share all the details. Otherwise, suspicions could grow, and a fight can break out later.

**Q.** One of our groomsmen is the only member of the wedding party without a spouse. He's been seeing a girl that I don't like very much—in fact, none of the guys do—and I'm afraid he might bring her as his "and guest." I don't want her sitting at the head table—in fact, I don't want her there at all. But I don't want him to be alone, either.

**A.** Unfortunately, you can't decide who he brings as his date, and you can't encourage him to leave his significant other at home. But you can arrange for yourself and your groom to sit at a sweetheart's table and seat your bridal party at other tables, so that you won't have to deal with her very much. Many couples are skipping the head table arrangement and allowing their bridal parties to sit among the guests in their own social circles. At the wedding, just focus on all the people who you're happy to have in attendance, and the others—like this unwelcome woman—will fade into the background.

# Chapter 4

# Getting the Groom in Gear

You're partnering on the wedding plans, and this is the first really big, emotionally loaded and financially straining event you've taken on together. You're busy with your careers, strapped for time, and you have a lot of outside opinions coming at you from your parents, your friends, and your wedding vendors. You're stressed, you're navigating the tricky path of building a relationship with your in-laws (which can get strangely convoluted when his parents get involved with the wedding plans, too), and, under all this pressure, you're dealing with each other in a way that's different from what you're used to. For instance, if you've taken the lead in planning the wedding, your fiancé might be understandably annoyed if you're delegating tasks to him and watching over his shoulder as he performs them. You don't mean to be "the boss." It's just that the wedding plans are important to you.

Especially if you both have different working styles—for instance, if you can't sleep unless your to-do list is checked off, while he's more laid back and leaves things undone—this may be the first time your different styles have bumped up against each other. Add in your different styles of coping with stress, and you may be snapping at one another or simmering in silent resentment when one is not as focused on the wedding details as the other. At the start of the wedding planning process, you may have agreed on what you'd work on together and separately, but as time went on and new developments emerged, his attitude changed, or you grew more intense about the little things. In the interest of good diplomacy, agree to keep your partnering flexible. If you initially agreed to make every Sunday morning wedding planning time, but your fiancé isn't happy about giving up golf time or you're not happy about giving up breakfasts with your friends, agree to change that rule to every other Sunday. Your flexibility on these things is the essence of good diplomacy. A diplomat knows that it's not an ideal situation when the person you're dealing with doesn't want to be there. So use that empathy, be willing to hear "no," and work together to reformulate your partnering plan along the way.

Good diplomacy is give-and-take, and nowhere is that more essential than in your relationship with your fiancé. Look back at the character traits essential to good diplomacy mentioned on pages x–xi, because they really come into play with this most important relationship.

**Q.** My fiancé said he wanted to partner fully with me on the wedding, but I've asked him to help with several things and he "doesn't have time." I think he's just not interested.

**A.** This is the most common diplomacy scenario: You're at different levels of urgency and priority with the wedding plans. Most often, you'll both need to move your "notches" closer to meeting in the middle. Assess your own urgency level. Do you expect your fiancé to help you get everything done in the first month of your engagement? Do you expect him to accomplish his assigned tasks within twenty-four hours? Accept that not all people are on the same wavelength when it comes to timing, and take a deep breath. All things in good time.

If your fiancé is truly slacking on the tasks he's agreed to handle or partner on with you, if it's been weeks, then it's time for a discussion. He has to know how you feel about this, and you have to know what's going on in his mind. He may not see the urgency, simply because he doesn't realize that the plans really do have to be set months and months before the wedding.

It's very bad diplomacy to start off with an accusation, so approach your fiancé without any kind of blame statement or guilt trip—don't say anything like, "Why are you stalling? Don't you care about the wedding?" Instead, focus on the solution.

"Hon, when do you have a little bit of time for us to talk briefly about setting up a new wedding planning schedule?" You're honoring his schedule and his mood by beginning by asking when he has time.

## Keeping the Peace

The key to successful diplomacy is timing. Try to give your words the best chance to work when the other party is open, relaxed, and ready to talk.

You've also made the topic safe for him. You didn't leave it open-ended by saying something like, "We have to talk about the wedding," since that mysterious phrasing can set off alarm bells with your fiancé. It's the equivalent of "we have to talk" in dating. When he gives you a date and time, such as "Thursday night after I get back from the gym," or "Sunday morning, we can talk over brunch," honor that agreement. If you say his timing is fine, and then you try to change it to a sooner time, the trust factor goes down. If you honor his schedule, he'll be more likely to honor yours.

When you're at your new planning summit, explain just what you described here as your dilemma. For example: "I'd like to set up a new planning schedule that works for both of us. I've felt frustrated lately because we have so many things to make decisions on, and when I come to you with a topic, you say you don't have time. We're both busy, and I wouldn't want you to feel like you have to make rushed decisions. So let's go through our planning tasks and decide when we'll handle each of these things."

During your negotiations, you may find that you're explaining to him exactly how the wedding industry works. This isn't his world, so don't imply any sense of judgment or talk to him like a child as you instruct. No one likes to feel inadequate or out of the loop, and no one likes to be lectured. As you explain the wedding industry's timing, let him know that you're learning about it right now too. "I just read an article in a bridal magazine that says we're supposed to book the limousines six months in advance, at least, since our wedding takes place during prom season. If we want the best cars at the best prices, we have to get on it by next month at the latest." Your informative tone works, since most men just want to get to the part where they have the facts and know what they need to do.

If he jokes or states that you have been too intense about the wedding plans lately, don't shut down your diplomacy with an irate "I have not been intense! It just seems that way since you're such a slacker!" Being able to laugh at yourself is a diplomacy strengthener, so you can just smile and shake your head with an "I know, I know, you got me. That's why we're making a new schedule now." As you plan the timing of your shared tasks, and set deadlines for your individual tasks, talk about any potential trade-offs. Guys love knowing they have an out if they find they really don't know too much about limousines or photography. And be open to his sharing your tasks with you. It may be far less threatening for him to shop with you for wedding favors than to be responsible for the wedding videographer arrangements.

Finally, figure out how you'd both like to be kept on schedule by the other. "If it's getting close to a deadline, or if it is a deadline, how would you like me to remind you to get on it?" sounds simplistic, but it really does work. Both brides and grooms say that it isn't the reminders that annoyed them, it was the daily e-mails, or how he or she always "got in my face right when I came home from work." Good diplomacy means finding the communication style that works for the other party, so agree right now that you'd like your reminders to be delivered in the form of a single e-mail or a note left on the counter.

**Q.** My fiancé is a little too invested in the wedding. He says that since we're paying for it, the wedding should reflect us . . . only he's going way overboard.

**A.** Brides get a bad rap sometimes, being called "Bridezillas" when there are plenty of grooms out there who have controlling, egomaniacal sides to their personalities, lack the ability to handle stress, and get quite anal about the plans.

If your fiancé is barking at you, stressing about the plans, or coming up with ideas that confuse or could potentially embarrass you (a *Monty Python and the Holy Grail*–themed wedding?), plan a relaxing evening for the two of you . . . serious time to unwind with a nice dinner, a bottle of wine, a great movie, or maybe a back rub or a foot rub—you know what works best for him. The key is to chill him out a little bit and approach the topic with humor.

Try this by saying: "Sweetie, you seem way, way stressed about the wedding plans." Then see what he says. He may come out with a sigh of agreement, or laugh with you about it, or confess that he really wants this wedding to reflect the two of you, and he just can't find the perfect vendor or specialty act that he has in mind. He might say that he's trying really hard to give you the wedding of your dreams on a lower budget that will put you both in a more comfortable financial position after the wedding, or that he's getting a lot of pressure from his mother to conform to the family's traditions. He didn't want to tell you about his mother's meddling, since he knows that sets you off, and he's sorry he's been so intense lately.

## Keeping the Peace

Very often, good diplomacy is in saying just a little bit . . . and then letting the other person talk.

Or he might say, "What? Me? Intense? No, I'm not." He really might not be aware that he's over-invested and just a little bit scary with his outbursts over the invitation fonts. It could be that he's operating on automatic. He's this intense over his work projects, which gets him rewarded at the office. This is the same scenario for a lot of brides who get super-intense about the wedding plans; some have no idea they're being inappropriate or dramatic. If your fiancé is in the dark about how his behavior affects you, let him know with concrete facts, not interpretations. For instance, look at this exchange:

**YOU:** "Yesterday, you got all mad because the border on the menu cards wasn't a pearlized border."

**HIM:** "I did? Well, it wasn't what we ordered."

**YOU:** "I agree, and we need to change it. But your getting so mad and throwing the sample to the floor concerned me."

Notice you're agreeing that a change needs to be made to the problem that sparked the outburst. And you're saying that his action concerned you, not that his reaction was immature, over-the-top, or any other judgment phrasing. And stick with "your getting mad" or "your getting upset," rather than going anywhere near "you looked like you were going to cry" or "your veins were bulging out of your neck!" Your fiancé needs to know that he's safe in expressing his feelings to you, and if you're condemning him now—especially if he wasn't aware that his reactions were intense—you could cause him to distance himself a little bit, hide his feelings, or stifle himself. Stick to the facts, and don't analyze him.

Keep in mind, though, that if your expressing your concern about his intensity and anger doesn't get him to see the issue and adjust his coping skills, you might want to sign up for premarital couples' counseling.

**Q.** My future mother-in-law is being very difficult, actually changing some of the plans I've made for the wedding, and my fiancé won't stand up for me. I've

**asked him to say no to her "requests," but he just shrugs and walks away.**

**A.** The dynamic between your fiancé and his mother is likely to be very complicated. Even if she's in the wrong about anything, "the good son" is going to stand up for her, or completely avoid standing up to her. Take a look at how situations have gone in the past, when you wanted him to stand up to her and it just didn't happen. Take those early experiences as "the way it is," and don't set yourself up for a lifetime of frustration by expecting him to morph into what you want him to be—that is, on your side all the time.

Some grooms, of course, do have a healthy level of distance from their mothers, are able to view a dilemma fairly from all sides, and have the assertiveness to speak to whoever is in the wrong. That may be you sometimes. If he does have a level of fairness and a calming, problem-solving influence, it could mean that he just doesn't see the intensity of this problem. It could be that you're asking him to wrangle her a little too often, or about too many things. The guy doesn't want to be in the middle, doesn't want anyone angry with him, or doesn't want to open up the can of worms that is a groom's dilemma: "Which of these two important women in my life do I support in this argument of theirs?" He may think he's in a no-win situation, and he just doesn't want to be in the situation at all.

You may see it as her trying to be the alpha-female of your wedding—overruling you, overruling your fiancé, and getting her way at any cost. Rather than wasting any time trying to analyze why she's like this, your good diplomacy leads you to find a solution. Stick to the top level of this situation, as digging deep or trying to reconstruct their relationship is only going to frustrate you.

Very likely, you have two main problems here—wanting your fiancé to join you in a united front, and wanting your future mother-in-law to respect your wedding plans and choices. The second will come after you arrange the first. Your diplomatic goal here, and it's a big one, is to bring your fiancé to a place where he understands your hurt feelings and will join you in a united front once the situation has been assessed as true fault on his mother's part. By that, I mean that you can explain the problem with facts—not that she uses a rude tone with you, or ignores your calls. Those kinds of things are interpretive. She might have been having a bad day, or she might have been on vacation and that's why she didn't return your call for a week.

Let's say your future mother-in-law called a vendor and changed a plan that you had already set. That's a fact. She made the call, and now the vendor shows that there's a new order for a traditional, white-frosted cake when you ordered a chocolate-frosted cake. With that fact in hand, you have every right to expect your fiancé to join you as a united front in approaching his mother to right the wrong.

This does not mean that he has to call her about the cake. Her action was taken against both of you. Whenever it's an act against the wedding, it's an act against both of you. So your fiancé should not be expected to fight this battle on his own. Here's your smart diplomatic start: "What's the best way for us to talk to your mother about her changing the cake order?" You're not asking if you should talk to his mother. You're stating that there will be a conversation, and you've used the word "us." Your fiancé may dread the upcoming conversation, as anyone would when dealing with a difficult parent, but you've just placed the dilemma at a much more effective starting point. You've also done so by stating the problem you're dealing with clearly, rather than citing some vague statement like "your mother is so difficult" or "your mother is such a [fill in the blank]."

If your fiancé attempts to shrug it off, preferring the disrespect to an impending confrontation with his mother, don't give up. That's just his first response, and many first responses are automatic. He may have been shrugging off his mother's bad behavior for years. He's reacting to this slight without any thought to just how bad it is, and just how badly it hurts you. You'll now use your diplomatic strengths to make it more clear to him.

"Come on, now. We can't just let this go. Neither of us wants a white-frosted cake, and it would be a very bad thing for us to let your mother boss us around without at least saying something about it. She absolutely has to hear a no from us on this, and we have to call and fix the cake order."

You're asserting your deepest feelings without delving into blame or saying anything that could hit that automatic defend-your-mother button that he has deep inside of him, and you're not going anywhere near the idea of making her fix the cake order. It's far better for you to just pick up the phone and apologize to the cake baker for the confusion, explain that your mother-in-law got confused about the cake order (better than saying "she's a control freak"), and change the order back to what you originally wanted.

As far as the meeting with his mother, do it in person if you can. Face-to-face discussions are always better than a phone chat, and way better than an e-mail. Before you go, though, practice with your fiancé. Start off that discussion with a preface: "I know this isn't pleasant for you. It's not pleasant for me either, since I really want to have a harmonious relationship with your entire family. But we can't let your mother make the decisions she's making, or she'll keep doing it after the wedding day, and you and I will have tension in our marriage over and over and over. I know you don't want that, so let's do something *now* so that we have a better chance of preventing future problems like this."

## Keeping the Peace

Face-to-face discussions are always better than a phone chat, and way better than an e-mail.

You've made some excellent points, as far as your fiancé is concerned. He's going to hear that this conversation may be tough, but it's going to prevent future confrontations like this and strengthen your relationship. Tell him, "It's important for our marriage that we are a united front. That's not the same as taking sides. It's honoring each other's feelings, which I would do for you."

You'll then practice what you're going to say, how you're going to phrase your requests to her, and how you'll handle her comebacks. Using your practice statements, the conversation might sound like this:

**YOU:** "We'd like to talk with you about the cake order." Not "what you did to our cake order," since that's a blame statement. You'd shut the conversation down right there.

**HER:** "What about the cake order?" Hmmm, she's pretty crafty. She's going to make you say it.

**YOU:** "The baker said you called and changed our cake order to white frosting, when we ordered a chocolate wedding cake." You don't flinch. You're stating the facts.

**FIANCÉ:** "We've changed the order back to what we ordered, and we have to ask you not to make changes to our wedding plans." He needs to look her in the eye and stick to the facts. She's going to be stunned, especially if he isn't quite in practice standing up to her.

**HER:** "Oh, really? You know, your father and I are spending a lot of money helping you out with this wedding.

Since it's not traditionally the case that the groom's family helps to pay, we could always take back our contribution."

Stop right here. She's bringing out the big guns, trying to scare you into letting her do things her way. If she makes this threat—and it is a threat—think about whether or not you can say, "Okay, fine" and refund her. That takes her power away. If you can't, ignore the threat and get back to your solution-focused conversation. If you don't respond to this statement, you won't let her lead you away from the facts and into an emotional battle. Or, you could turn the threat back on her, but in a good way:

**FIANCÉ:** "We hope you won't be one of those parents who actually makes that kind of threat. That's not like you."

**HER:** "We? Darling"—to her son—"did she put you up to this?" And now she's trying divide and conquer. If your fiancé looks like he's going to fold, just touch his arm for support. Grabbing his hand and holding it is more of an Animal Planet–like maneuver to show dominance over the mother, so that's not needed. You don't want to physically embody the loyalty game she fears.

**FIANCÉ:** "[Your name] didn't put me up to anything." He's not going to call you "she" as a matter of respect, since you're in the room. "We both agree that it was

wrong of you to call the baker to change the cake order."
Avoid the whole "behind our backs" thing. Again, stick
to the facts. "And we'd like you to agree not to make
that kind of mistake again."

It might take a few back and forths, and your future
mother-in-law is going to use every tool she has, perhaps even bursting into tears, which she knows will
guilt trip her son. You're not cold, so a bit of empathy
for her is going to go a long way.

**YOU:** "We'd really like for our wedding planning process to be something we can share with our entire families, and I'd personally like a very harmonious relationship with your family. We appreciate everything you've
done for the wedding so far, but can we agree that if
you'd like any changes to the plans, you'll call one of
us first?"

You've done the best you can. Keep this visit short. When
you've gotten to a workable solution, get out of there before
any other new problem can surface. Thank his mother for listening to you both. You've just taken the first step of many
toward creating a positive relationship among all of you. I say
"first step" quite intentionally, as it may take a long time and
many efforts to get the message through to her. If you keep
your united front and stick to the facts, confront her together
rather than expecting your fiancé to be the middle man, you'll
work your way toward success. And your fiancé will be more

willing to partner with you on his mother's antics in the future when this meeting goes better than he expected.

**Q.** We're at odds about the cost of the wedding. We have a budget, and he wants to stick to the guesses we made at the start of the process, not a penny over. I'd like to be more fluid and change amounts, taking from some less-valued portions and putting more money into the things I really want. We're clashing over money.

**A.** First, find out why your fiancé wants to stick so rigidly to a plan you made before you had any real, in-depth experience in your wedding plans. You can't solve his problem if you don't know why he's clinging so strongly to your initial guesses. It may be that the budget has grown out of control, and he's looking at every penny. He might also need to understand why you want to be more fluid with the budget, so try this approach:

"I'd like to shift our budget around a little bit, take what we have and devote a larger percentage to the reception than to the flowers. We started off with guesses about what things would cost, and I think we're doing a good job of staying within our limits. Now that I've seen more caterers' menus and prices, I really think it would allow us to get a much better meal for our guests if we put [dollar amount] into that, while we cut [dollar amount] from the flower budget." You've explained how it works. He might not have understood the concept of being more fluid with the budget. To him, it might have sounded like you wanted to be more fluid in terms of cashing in your IRAs and savings accounts to buy more wedding stuff. Restate your wishes in another way to make sure he gets the picture.

If he still wants to stick with the original budget, it might be a way for him to feel like he has a handle on such a big expense. If a change is made anywhere, he might fear that everything will spin out of control. So here is your script: "Take a look at the wedding expense averages in our area, which I found on *www.costofwedding.com*. You'll see where we're spending less than the area average, and how close we are to average. We're not adding more expense to the budget, but rather just changing the percentages." As true financial partners, disclosure is essential, so share with him exactly which categories you'll increase the budget for, and which will get less money. Your closing script: "Are you okay with that arrangement before we make any changes?"

With a fact-centric discussion, you'll find that diplomacy has paved the way for a more productive financial plan.

**Q.** My fiancé isn't wild about my friends, and the feeling is mostly mutual, so I'd like to ask him to be cordial at our pre-wedding parties.

**A.** You just want peace between your intended and your friends, so preface any pre-wedding parties, right before the parties, with a kindhearted reminder.

"Now, I know that you're not wild about my friends," and there's no need to even mention that they're not wild about him, "but please—for me—just peacefully coexist with them tonight. If you would like a rescue from Sally," who is notoriously chatty or critical, "just tug on your earlobe, and I'll come over to run interference." No need to go into how you're polite to his rude friends at parties, as this is not a competition. Don't shut down your odds of success by mentioning anything controversial or anything he feels he needs to defend. Just give him this straight request, with a message that you're looking out for him.

**Q.** I've been stressed over the wedding plans, and he's pulled away, spending more time with his friends when I'd rather he just relax with me. We really need to focus on our relationship, but he seems to be staying away. He says it's for "his protection."

**A.** If he's like most grooms-to-be, he's half kidding/half serious about it being safer for him to distance himself from you a little bit. If you've been stressed about the wedding plans, even if it's straight-up stressed and not stressed to the point of being dramatic, obnoxious, and snappy, you're not entirely the person he knows and loves. Let's assume that's the case, and if you admit that you've been a little difficult lately, then you can understand where your fiancé is coming from. Many men tell me that they have stressful lives already with the pressures of work, busy social schedules, financial pres-

sures, and even feel run-down with this new job—and planning a wedding is a job—added to their lives. It's a disruption
of his schedule, just as it has been for yours, and he may not
have time to work out or unwind fully. So we'll chalk this one
up to your fiancé needing a little space to recharge, which definitely is in order. If it was you in a state of overwhelm, you'd
probably want to distance yourself from a high-energy person
coming at you with endless details, questions, and timelines.

Understanding his point of view is only a part of it, though.
You still have needs that aren't being met. Approach him with
the following script: "Even in the middle of this wedding
planning process, I really crave closeness with you, and we
need time to nurture our relationship." So approach him with
an offer, one that leaves out what you might think are essential
points. You won't start off by saying how distant he's been or
how it hurts your feelings that he's joking about you being
stressed. Instead, go more diplomatic with your solution-only
offer by saying: "I'd like for us to spend more time together.
With the wedding coming up, I've been a bit stressed, and it
would calm me so much more if we could just have dinner
or sit on the couch and watch a movie, or go to a comedy
club like we've always done, give each other backrubs, and
have lots of great sex." Seriously, is he going to say no to that?
"We'll make these no-wedding-talk-allowed dates, which I'd
really love to have with you." You haven't mentioned one thing
about how he prefers to spend time with his friends rather
than with you, since that's a diplomacy killer and is likely to
get you an ill-timed joke about how his friends aren't losing

their minds like you are. So don't even mention the friends, or his time on the golf course. A man will hear that as: "You're not doing enough for me," which—if he's overwhelmed and stressed—is the last thing he wants to hear.

**Q.** When I try to talk with my fiancé about the wedding, he just says "Whatever you want, it's your day." I'm hurt by his indifference.

**A.** While more than 80 percent of grooms are full planning partners in wedding preparation, some sign on halfheartedly. Your fiancé knows it's important to you to have him on board, and in the initial flush of excitement over the engagement, he agreed to partner with you. Don't worry, I'm not going to say you should let him off the hook or fire him. Step one in diplomacy is trying to understand where his behavior is coming from. Maybe he's traditional and really feels like a wedding is for the bride to plan. Many well-meaning grooms take the position that they just want to give the bride everything she wants her way, since it's so important to her. So think about the times he has said, "whatever you want, it's your day." Did you hear an indifference that's not really there? It could be your fear coloring that moment in your memory. He could truly want you to have everything your way. It's highly unlikely that he doesn't care.

It could be that he's unsure of how you'll accept his suggestions. You might think it's nothing that you laughed when he suggested purple for the color theme, in homage to your alma mater. That idea may have meant a lot to him, but he took a risk and got shot down. So, in fact, your fiancé might have read those instances as your wanting and needing to have everything your way. Not in the sense that you're a control freak, but that this wedding and every detail therein is very, very important to you. And that you already know everything you want.

To solve this issue with great diplomacy, ask him for a good time to talk, and come prepared with a request that's direct and to-the-point. Try saying: "I love it that you want me to have the wedding of my dreams, and a big part of my dream is planning it with you. So let's sit down here and talk about some of the details, like the catering. I really want to know what you'd like to have on the menu. We can choose eight appetizers, so why don't you pick four and I'll pick four." Given a direct request like that, most grooms would be happy to pick four delicious menu items off of a list.

It could be that you haven't been presenting wedding planning tasks in a way that's friendly to him. He may not have responded to "what kind of food do you want?" as that's a much larger topic. When you find the secret code that appeals to your fiancé—being quick and to-the-point, giving him choices off of a list, and so on—you may find that he's more interested in participating.

**Q.** **My fiancé is telling everyone how much we're spending on the wedding, like it makes him a bigger guy. This is really embarrassing me.**

**A.** It's a tough thing to tell your fiancé, who is an adult, that his behavior is embarrassing you, so forget the blame. Just say: "Sweetie, I noticed a few people with blank looks on their faces as you were talking about the wedding budget." You're not saying the people rolled their eyes at him. "Why don't we agree not to talk about our personal financial plans for the wedding with anyone else? It just seems like our friends would be more comfortable if we avoid the topic."

Now, if you have joined in on the info-sharing in your initial engagement excitement, you can preempt his calling you a hypocrite by sharing your thoughts: "I know, I've been doing it too, but I'm only just noticing that no one seems to enjoy hearing about that part of our wedding plans. So I'm going to stop bragging, or complaining, about how much everything costs." If you go into how you've decided to spare others' feelings when they're having more modest weddings, that puts you dangerously close to martyr territory, and promoting yourself as the model for good behavior isn't quite the diplomatic solution. Be aware of how you make this request, and tell him it means a lot to you.

**Q.** My fiancé keeps adding people to the guest list, like colleagues and old friends he's never mentioned before—way too many people.

**A.** The possible reasons for a man's additions to a guest list are too many to analyze here—maybe he wants more people from his side to equal the number of people on your side, maybe wants to connect with old friends, impress his bosses and colleagues, adhere to a code at work that says all bosses and colleagues are invited to weddings (he would be the only guy in the office not to), and so on. Whatever the reason, he just keeps writing down more names. With your limited budget and smallish wedding celebration space, you just won't be able to accommodate these not-so-close invitees. But how to tell him?

"We need to go through the guest list and cut it down a bit so that we can keep it to a manageable size and not spend a fortune on the wedding. I know you'd like to have more people from your office and from your school days at the wedding, so let's make a plan on how we're going to work this. What do you think about us both including all of our bosses and closest colleagues, but limit our friends only to people we get together with and those we speak to often—our closest friends only?"

You'll have to be ready for give-and-take as well, and both of you need to be ready for one side of the family to out-number the other. You might come from a large family while he only has a handful of cousins, aunts, and uncles. Assure him that there will never be a moment at the wedding where his side will be corralled into one area, thus spotlighting the difference in headcount. You'll have the ushers seat more of your guests on his side, and the guest tables will be mixed at the reception. That usually solves the comparison dilemma.

If this is a case of your fiancé wanting to connect with old friends, remind him that his class reunion is coming up in a year, and that he'll see them all there, just as you'll see all your old school friends at your reunion rather than inviting them to the wedding. "Besides, we'll be so busy on the wedding day that we won't really get a chance to mingle for very long with all of our guests."

Avoid judging his guest list with your take on who is worthy to be invited and who is not. Stay away from criticisms like "They didn't send you a Christmas card this year, and you want to invite them?" Avoid the measuring and stick with your goal—getting to a head count that works for your size and budget, which may require you to cut some of your own distant relatives and so-so friends to make room for more of his wished-for relatives. Your thoughtfulness will go a long way.

And, of course, create a B-list of people you'll invite if your top-tier guests respond that they can't attend. It's smart to send out your invitations early, as most "no" responses will come in right away from those who know they have vacation plans or work requirements then.

**Q.** My fiancé wants to invite his ex-girlfriend, with whom he's still friends, to the wedding. She flirts with him like crazy, and I don't want her there.

**A.** He's still friends with her, and as much as I'd love to be able to say it's diplomatic for you both to have veto power over each others' guest list choices, this one could backfire. Here's why: If you lay down the law about her not getting on the guest list, he's likely to talk with this friend of his, apologizing to her that you don't want her there. He'll be comforting her, and depending on how much of a manipulator she is, he might just feel the need to take her out to dinner to make her feel better. Your trying to keep her from the wedding gives her a great, big, honking message: You're afraid of her. And it could give them time alone, which would be worse than having her be one of 200 people at your wedding. So my best advice is to remember your self-confidence and the strength of your relationship with your fiancé. Be the bigger person, and don't say anything about her being invited. Look at what a decent guy your fiancé is, that he can be friends with his ex, and that he has never been receptive to her flirting. She may just be an insecure woman who flirts with everyone; maybe she's dying for attention. The wedding day is all about you and your groom, and he will only be thinking about that.

If, at the wedding, this ex-girlfriend does flirt with your groom, stride right up to her and say, "Wow, that's a lot of hair flipping and touching his arm." You're stating the facts with a smile, not snarling, and then you lead your husband away by asking him to come say hello to guests or to dance with you.

Take the high road, the diplomatic road, and resist the urge to tell this rude girl off. Who flirts with the groom? A desperate woman who is interested in playing games and who measures her power by how many heads she can turn. Just don't overreact to her talking to him. They are friends. But you can tell the difference between a chat of congratulations and "dome" eyes and lots of touching. She'll find a bartender to flirt with in a few minutes flat.

**Q.** My fiancé doesn't want me to invite my ex-boyfriend, with whom I'm still friends.

**A.** Of course, this issue goes both ways. If you have an ex-boyfriend with whom you're still friends—even if you know there's absolutely nothing flirtatious between you—you can probably empathize with your fiancé's discomfort at having this guy around. After all, he slept with you. Visual people don't like to have that reminder in the room, and that's a fact.

To handle this dilemma, just explain that "He and I have been friends for a long time. I'm close with his family, and we only dated for a few months in college. I know it's a hot button for you, but I'd really like for him to be at the wedding. I hope you won't ask me to leave him off the list, since that would be unpleasant for me to have to do. He has a fiancée now, and he's very happy with her." That ought to do it.

What if you dated the ex for a long time and were very serious with him? It takes a very secure partner not to feel at least a twinge over that one. This is a guy you were in love with, after all. Aren't there some memories swimming around in your head? When the relationship was more serious, empathize with your fiancé with the following: "Honey, I know you don't like the idea of him being at the wedding, but let me assure you that I was never as happy with him as I am with you. I never think about the old days with him, since you give me so much to think about now. The past is the past. I'm marrying you."

Think about what you would like your fiancé to say to you if the tables were turned. What would make you feel more secure? Keep it short, or your efforts here will backfire. Your fiancé will dislike your going on and on about how your ex means absolutely nothing to you and he doesn't have to worry—your man may sense that you feel he needs validation. The simpler the statement, the better.

**Q.** **My fiancé is angry that the wedding has gotten so big and so expensive, and he wants us to cancel and just do a small destination wedding. I know it would be smarter financially, but I don't want to give up my dream of a big, formal wedding.**

**A.** That's exactly what you should say. With a tilt of your head and a smile, not in a whiny or angry tone: "I know that things have gotten out of hand, but I'd really be disappointed to have an entirely different wedding than the one I've had my heart set on. Instead, let's look at how we can carve out some of the extra expenses from the wedding plans and cut down the guest list a bunch. We don't need 400 people there, so we'll draw the line at first cousins. I'll get a book on budget-saving ideas, and we'll make lots of changes. I agree with you totally. The budget is way too big, and I know we agree that we don't want a circus. So let's look at all the ways we can improve things." You're solution-focused and willing to make sacrifices. Most grooms who have made this declaration have done so because they didn't think their brides would be willing to shrink down their wedding plans. Also, many grooms say they declare this out of frustration and are very pleased with the changes they make together with their brides.

**Q.** I got suckered by a shady vendor with a bad contract. I feel awful about it, and my fiancé doesn't want me to handle any more of the wedding bookings.

**A.** No one ever feels great about getting suckered, and no one feels great about getting punished afterward. Sure, there may have been some red flags you missed, but the shady vendor is at fault here. This scenario could tempt you to get very, very angry at your fiancé and to state all the times you did handle contracts well, that you're an educated professional, and so on. But that accomplishes nothing, diplomacy-wise. Your fiancé might not intend to restrict you from handling the vendors' contracts, and there might not be an intended insult about your ability to tackle the business end. It might be that he saw how stressed and upset you got at that vendor, and he wants to spare you any future stress or anger. So don't fuel the problem by attaching meanings to his decision. That's not productive. With your best diplomatic smarts, just go to your fiancé and explain the following calmly, rationally, and with confidence.

**YOU:** "Honey, I know that you're only trying to protect me by taking over the vendors' contracts." You're giving him the benefit of the doubt. "But I'm feeling like you don't have much confidence in my ability to handle them. I doubt we'll run into another vendor as shady as that guy was, so I'd like to handle the contracts for the florist, photographer, and videographer, since I've already met with them and described what we wanted." You're not asking permission, you're stating what you want.

**YOUR FIANCÉ:** "Don't worry, I'll handle it." Pat on the head optional. At this point, respond with the help of this script:

**YOU:** "I know that you're just looking out for me, but I'm uncomfortable with this arrangement. It makes me feel very much like a subordinate, and I'd like for my one mistake not to live on in the future. The guy lied to me, and it makes me very angry to think about that. This arrangement where you handle the contracts is a daily reminder of how someone ripped me off and took advantage of my good nature, and I know you don't want me to feel awful all the time. If I'm handling contracts with good vendors, that would make me really happy."

Notice I said, "this arrangement," not "your taking this job away from me."

This scenario is a great learning exercise for the conflicts you'll face together in the future. When your fiancé shows faith in you, that strengthens your partnership.

## Keeping the Peace

Blame isn't going to move you forward. It's going to shut down diplomatic negotiations.

**Q.** We're writing our wedding vows, and he won't read them to me before the wedding. I know he has kind of a smart-aleck sense of humor that not everybody gets, and I don't want him to offend anyone or embarrass me.

**A.** You have to honor his request to have the vows be a surprise to you at the wedding. Obviously, he's worked on them, he's proud of them, and he has every right to have his vows be a reflection of his personality as well. You believe he has a smart-aleck sense of humor, and you think that's what he's trying to hide. It could be that he's written something very sentimental, and he wants you to hear it for the first time at the ceremony. His wanting privacy doesn't mean he's going to start reciting limericks. If he does have his trademark sense of humor in his vows, that's his style. Here's one factor that could make you feel better: Many officiants, especially those in a house of worship, require that you share your wedding vows with them for their approval before the wedding day. If anything is truly off-color in his vows, the officiant can nix that particular part.

A wedding coordinator can also offer to read both of your vows ahead of time, just for the sake of timing and coordination, some editorial suggestion, and offering tips on great delivery. Crisis averted. No diplomatic wording is needed here, other than, "We're both supposed to run our vows by the officiant for approval, and [wedding coordinator] also offered to listen to our first drafts. They've both promised to keep our vows confidential." You've worded it as a task to be done, not a vague "if you want to."

**Q.** My fiancé is really nervous about marriage since his parents are divorced. The closer the wedding gets, the more freaked out he's becoming.

**A.** This is a case for premarital counseling; it's not a situation that you can handle with a wise, diplomatic statement to your fiancé. Fears and stress are best handled by professionals, and you can sign on for short-term counseling with a highly recommended expert. He or she will guide you both through discussions about what you expect from the marriage, as well as create a game plan for handling any conflicts in the future. Going to counseling is a great investment in your marriage, getting you to focus on the larger issues as you work through any exercises or read any books "prescribed" to you. Now, what is the best way to suggest counseling to your partner? This may be the diplomatic hurdle, as your fiancé might be concerned about spending extra money or about the stigma of needing counseling.

Don't try to read his mind by prefacing the discussion with, "We won't tell anyone we're going." That could actually plant the idea that going to counseling is something to hide or be ashamed of. So treat it as the beneficial step that it is, and tell your partner what you'd like to address in the sessions, as you have some pre-wedding jitters too. That's way better than allowing him to feel like you're both going because of a problem he's having.

Try saying: "We're just enlisting the advice of a professional in the same way we're hiring experts in flowers, entertainment, and photography for the wedding. It's short-term—only once a week for six weeks—and I think it would be terrific for us to invest in our future, not just the wedding. What do you think? I'd really like to do it, since I've read so much in the bridal magazines about premarital counseling being the thing to do." Your fiancé has just heard the benefits, and that it's something lots of couples are doing.

# Chapter 5

# Vendors with an Attitude

While you have the ideas and wishes for your wedding, your vendors are the experts who will bring everything to life. You need these people to create everything from your bouquets to each exquisite dish on your menu, the décor, fabulous photographs—all of the elements of your wedding. They're crucial to the success of your day, and to you getting everything you hoped for. So what happens when you have problems with these people? What happens when you're in awe of, and perhaps a little bit intimidated by, that cake baker, or that florist, with all of his or her creative genius, a celebrity flair, a photo feature spread in *InStyle Weddings*, and awards for being the best in his or her industry . . . and you don't like where your planning process is going? What happens if you don't like the expert after the first two meetings, but you're locked in by a contract?

You can't cut and run, or you'll lose your deposit. You feel like you can't say, "Hey, buddy, you work for me!" without fearing that he'll deliver wilted flowers or less-than-stellar appetizers for your wedding.

Handling your wedding vendors takes a skilled sense of professional-level diplomacy. It's a bit different from the diplomacy you use with your bridesmaids or with your parents, since those scenarios arise out of longtime, multilayered relationships—and you'll be dealing with those people in your future. With your wedding vendors, by contrast, you don't have a history with them—which is very often a good thing. It's just you and the expert, as wedding couple and wedding vendor, starting with a blank slate and focused only on partnering on your chosen wedding projects. But you are the boss, and the vendor does work for you.

The key to good diplomacy is to still treat the vendor as an equal, to realize that you both have the same goal—to achieve your wedding wish—even if you have different working or personality styles.

You'd be surprised at how many brides and grooms fear questioning or instructing their wedding vendors. When that's the case, the wedding couple becomes the problem. The vendor wants your instruction and guidance, because by making you happy, he or she will net referrals to a dozen of your other engaged friends. That's the strength of your position, but it isn't to be abused. It doesn't give you license to treat the vendor like he's your servant, demand rush service, change your mind incessantly, and expect him to magically produce a new cake with a day's notice.

The more rapport you can establish with a vendor, the better for both of you. And when problems crop up, as is normal when two people who don't know each other partner on such an important venture, you'll be able to handle them with wonderful diplomacy because you've built a foundation of mutual respect. So work on that rapport now, even if you're already feeling a few issues growing between you.

**Q.** **Our florist is pushing his ideas on us and telling us our ideas won't work.**

**A.** It's frustrating when a vendor says no—or "dares" to say no, as it might seem to you. But before you get too steamed, find out why the vendor doesn't think your ideas will work. If your wedding will be outdoors in the summer months, for instance, delicate flowers will wilt too easily. Sometimes a vendor is applying years of experience to a design idea, and his or her advice is right, even if it's something you don't want to hear. It might be that your choices don't work with the budget you've stated. A vendor doesn't like saying no, but the good ones would rather be honest with you about your limitations than allow you to order what you want and have a less-than-gorgeous final product. The expert is doing you a favor.

If it's a matter of style, however, that's another story. When you have differing visions, it's yours that counts. It's good diplomacy to say, "With all due respect, we know our choice might seem quirky to you, but it's what we would like." Experts like working with couples who are very clear about what they want. The more assertive you can be, respectfully, the better for all of you.

When a vendor is one of those prima donna types who knows everything and overrules your wishes with a dismissive kind of approach to you—"Trust me, I've been doing this for twenty years, I know what I'm doing"—this expert isn't fulfilling his or her promises to you . . . and is probably violating the customer service codes of the professional association to which he or she belongs. This one takes a face-to-face discussion, not an e-mail. Call and make an appointment to talk with the vendor, and come prepared with a clear statement of what you don't like as well as what you would like.

For the what-you-don't-like portion of your discussion, keep it very short and to the point. "We don't feel like our ideas are being heard," works very well, while "You're not listening to us!" is not going to work. Vendors don't respond well to juvenile complaints or to threats: "If you don't start listening to us, we're going to tell everyone we know how awful you are at this! And we know people who work for the newspaper, too!" That's bullying, not diplomacy, and more wedding vendors have started filing restraining orders against angry, threatening clients. Stick to a general statement on why you're there to discuss a change in the dynamic of your partnership.

**YOU:** "We have some pictures here that we'd like to share with you. These centerpieces are a good example of what we'd like, only we'd like them to be smaller than shown here." When your vendor doesn't seem to get the picture, show a picture. A visual is the best way to prevent miscommunication, and a vendor with his or her own style can't argue with a client's specific request.

**VENDOR:** "That's not going to work with your reception style."

Find out why.

**YOU:** "Can you explain to us why our chosen center-pieces will not work for our wedding location, so that we can talk about what kind of alterations will make it work? Maybe a few colorful flowers tucked around those cacti would be perfection, or maybe we can choose another green, unique plant instead. But we're not going with daisies, as pretty as your sample photos are. Daisies are just not our style. Thanks."

There's no need to shake your contract at the vendor, or remind him that you outrank him. Stick to a method of listening to what doesn't work, and asking directly what can be done to *make* it work.

**Q.** Whenever we meet with our wedding coordinator she speeds through our to-do list, then rushes us out of the room.

**A.** You absolutely do deserve your wedding coordinator's undivided attention when you have an appointment. Yes, she's very busy and much in demand. Keep in mind that, if she has a wedding taking place that weekend, she may be working eighteen-hour days to pull that one off. But she's taken you on as a client, so she needs to make time for you. If you find that she's rushing through your to-do list during a meeting, show understanding and respect for her schedule:

"We have a ton of questions, and it seems like you're very rushed today. Can we reschedule for a time when you can block off a good hour to work on our wedding?" She will likely be hugely relieved, since 95 percent of her clients wouldn't show much care for her busy schedule. You're making her happy, but you're also making the best move for the success of your own wedding. She'll appreciate your offer to reschedule and she'll consider you one of her favorite clients—and wedding coordinators tell me they like to throw in some extras and favors for their favorite clients.

The key, for you, is finding a day and time that works best for her. "Which day of the week is your least busy?" Many coordinators take Mondays off after working a wedding, so their Tuesdays are just insane. Wednesdays might be the calmer day of the week for them. "Are you busier in the morning, at lunchtime, or at night?" Some coordinators are morning people. They know they're at peak performance between 6 a.m. and 10 a.m., so they jam their schedules. If you can grab a lunchtime appointment instead of an evening appointment, when the coordinator is exhausted or behind schedule, all the better. Your diplomacy here lies in finding out what works best for her. If she has the time to focus on you, then you'll get the service she's known for.

## Keeping the Peace

Don't expect a wedding coordinator to focus on your event 24/7 throughout the entire year before your wedding. Some have systems where they set the foundation of a wedding early in the process, and then you don't get switched into full-focus gear until three months before the wedding. The sooner you accept a wedding coordinator's system, the better. Ask for the date when she will elevate your event to full-access status.

**Q.** Our wedding coordinator handed us off to her assistant, since we have a smaller wedding. We didn't interview this assistant, we interviewed the wedding coordinator. How can we get her to take on our wedding?

**A.** Sometimes wedding coordinators hand off the beginning stages of a wedding to an assistant who is perfectly capable of taking notes from you, rounding up vendor bro-chures, and handling other administrative tasks. Before you get upset, ask the coordinator—phone or e-mail is fine—if this is the case.

Just say: "While we're happy with the initial planning steps your assistant has taken on our behalf, we're looking forward to working with you. When will you be joining us in working on our wedding plans?" There's no need to go into how you chose her instead of so many other coordinators, as that's just an indirect attempt at guilt tripping and manipulation. The coordinator knows you chose her. And she trusts her assistant to handle your details well for now. Your e-mail is respectful of her schedule, but still points out that you're looking for-ward to working directly with her.

If she responds with news that her assistant has been assigned to your wedding, you're in your full rights to turn down that arrangement. Again, you didn't interview the assis-tant. Your response, then, would be:

"While we're pleased with [assistant's] initial work, we'd like to stick with you as our wedding coordinator. When can we meet with you to continue the process?"

This pleasant and direct request should get you the meet-ing and should get you switched on to the coordinator's full-access plan. Coordinators say they appreciate a couple being assertive in a friendly way like this. The couple earns respect points from the planner, and, very often, the couple gets on the coordinator's project list.

If the coordinator says, however, that her assistant will be handling your wedding, since she's so busy with a big wedding, or the assistant handles your style of wedding, then this is a situation that you must handle with good diplomacy. Done badly, such as with a threat or with complaints about how you hired *her* and not the assistant, and you may get less than the 110 percent she gives to her best clients.

Say: "While we understand that you have full confidence in your assistant, we chose you because we attended the wedding you did for our friends and saw the great style that you have, and that's why we chose you to design our wedding. So we have to ask that you, and not your assistant, handle our wedding. We've enjoyed our conversations with her, but we have no examples of her work, and our wedding is just too important to work on with someone we didn't interview or hire." That's direct and to the point, and it should get you results.

You wedding coordinator may say: "Well, my schedule is full, so it's either my assistant or nothing." If you signed on the dotted line to have her plan your wedding, she's in breach of contract and you should be able to get all of your money back. (Hopefully, you read the contract's fine print and there's nothing in there about agreeing to have an assistant handle your wedding if the coordinator is unable to do so.) See the entry at the end of this chapter for the best, most diplomatic way to remove a bad vendor from your world.

**Q.** How can we approach our vendors with a request to get their services in exchange for advertising?

**A.** No doubt you've read about couples who got their flowers, cakes, tuxes, and other items for free—some couples have gotten their entire weddings for free—in exchange for advertising their vendors to all of their wedding guests. With the average wedding cost at around $40,000, the allure of this arrangement is quite understandable. After all, vendors get the chance to show their stuff to your 300 guests, possibly raking in dozens more events and weddings, and you get everything for free. While some couples find it tacky to arrange such a thing, not wanting to expose their guests to shameless plugs or have their wedding vows sponsored by Taco Bell, others have found more subtle ways to arrange service-for-exposure. They might offer the vendors space in their wedding programs, or allow their vendors to set out their business cards, such as a florist's cards available by the gorgeous arrangement in the cocktail party room.

Some couples are afraid of offending their vendors with the question alone. Others fear looking cheap, and then having the vendor refuse to work with them if the answer is no. So here is your script:

**YOU:** "We're looking into the new trend of services-for-exposure," is how you'll begin. You haven't asked them to work for free, and you haven't offended them.

150

**VENDOR:** "We've been asked about that by a lot of couples, and we'll only do it for weddings of more than 200 guests." Or, "No, we don't do that kind of arrangement, as we've found that we don't get enough interest from wedding guests. Too many of them are from out of town." Your answer has just come to you.

If the vendor doesn't volunteer information, then you can continue:

**YOU:** "We'd like to find out if and how we can arrange a services-for-exposure package with you. Have you done this in the past?"

The yes may be enthusiastic; the no may be the finale of the conversation. If they're interested, you can continue with:

**YOU:** "The brides and grooms we spoke to said that they offered their vendors a half-page ad in their programs, displayed the expert's signage at the table, and set out business cards. We'd be happy to do those same things for you, in exchange for your services." Some brides and grooms are able to offer some higher-level perks: Their wedding is going to be written up in a regional bridal magazine or in the newspaper, in an alumni newsletter, or in the society pages.

The promise of extensive promotional opportunities makes this proposal of yours an attractive offer to many vendors who depend on word of mouth for their success in a crowded and competitive industry. The vendor will respond in any number of ways, depending on his or her take on this whole services-for-exposure trend. The vendor may politely turn you down and hand you his price sheet, getting your conversation back to the point where he may get some cash out of you. But you asked in the most diplomatic way possible, you didn't try to connive anything, and you didn't burn a bridge.

**Q.** How can we ask our vendors for freebies and add-ons without seeming greedy?

**A.** Vendors don't think lowly of brides and grooms who ask for add-ons and freebies. They see you as savvy negotiators who know your bargaining strength and are just doing good business. It all depends on how you ask, of course.

"Given that we're booking you for the cocktail party, reception, and after-party, can we get your linen rental package for free?" is a smart, diplomatic request. If you're planning a $50,000 wedding, $500 in linen rentals is a breeze to a smart vendor who knows that you'll share this news with all of your friends. Always ask for the smaller things for free, of course. Some examples would be a free tux for your fiancé if your bridal party is renting twelve of them, a free parents' photo album from your photographer, or free use of the church organist considering that you'll tip him. You attract success in your requests for freebies when you've established a friendly and professional rapport with your experts, timed your request well, and asked for something of reasonable size and value.

## Keeping the Peace

One quick way to fail at this: tell them that your friend got freebies from them, and you demand the same. Some vendors deal with so many difficult brides and grooms that they'll turn down a request if you even unintentionally act like you're trying to rip them off.

**Q.** How can we negotiate things out of our vendors' packages?

**A.** As you're looking through the vendors' contracts with your vendor—and please do take the time to do this—or even if you're reviewing a contract you've wisely taken home to review, simply state, "Since we're not having an outdoor wedding, we'd like to take out this charge for rain delay services and extra movers." One place where you'll find lots of these is in your banquet hall's contract. These places routinely claim charges for cake-cutting (sometimes $1.50 to $2.00 per slice, called a "plating fee" or a "cutting fee"), and for opening each bottle of wine (called a "corkage fee"). If you haven't heard of these things, your jaw may be hanging open right now. Yes, they're tricky little add-on charges that are completely ridiculous when you consider how many thousands of dollars you're spending to have your wedding at their establishment.

Simple statements such as "We'd like to eliminate the cake-cutting fee" or "We'd like to take out the corkage fee" are your best diplomatic statements. Make sure to look the vendor in the eye—it doesn't work quite so well if you keep your eyes on the contract and make the request. That doesn't show confidence. Most vendors will strike these charges when you state it like this, although if they start to refuse, you can smile and say, "Come on, now. We have the platinum package with you, and we'd appreciate it if you'd do us this favor."

Your vendor may say that their contracts are nonnegotiable. Some vendors do stick to that with an iron fist, but you can and should still try. If you don't want an ice sculpture as the service style for your clams casino and shrimp cocktail, just say "We find ice sculptures to be a little too bridal, so we'd prefer that the seafood just be served on regular platters. It says here that the ice sculpture service style is $150, so we'd like to have that removed." They can't force you to have the ice sculpture if you don't want it. Again, it's all in your friendly demeanor—make your request respectfully and look them in the eye.

**Q.** Our cake baker hasn't returned our phone calls for weeks, and our site manager is now a week late returning our calls. How can we get them to be more timely and respectful?

**A.** Late return of calls seems to be an epidemic in our society, as everyone is working so hard, and wedding vendors are taking on extra clients in this busy time of more weddings per season. Give the vendors the benefit of the doubt, focusing on finding a solution instead of getting offended. If the cake baker isn't returning calls, and if you live nearby, stop in and try to catch the cake baker during the day. Not in a kick-the-door-down-and-demand-service kind of way, but rather in an I-was-just-in-the-neighborhood kind of way. As Woody Allen said, "Ninety percent of success is just showing up," and that applies to working with vendors. You may have more success when you're right there, in person, with a smile on your face. You should be respectful of their schedules, and not force them to sit down with you for a tasting or consultation on your time. You're showing up to get some face time, remind them that it's a pleasure working with you, and either get your questions answered quickly or set up an appointment for that tasting.

If you don't live nearby, but someone you trust does, ask them to stop in on your behalf. Not with a reproach—"You haven't called my daughter back, you jerk!"—but rather with a smile and a disarming, "I'm just helping out the bride and groom, and I'd love to get a copy of your fillings selection sheet for them. Thank you." Charm and respect go a long way. That cake baker will likely hand over that fillings sheet that you've been trying to get through weekly phone calls.

If you can't get to the vendor, and you have no helpers in the area, then you'll need to leave a stronger message with the vendor's assistant: "I've been trying to get through to [vendor] for three weeks now, and I'm getting very frustrated that I haven't been called back. I know she's busy, but our wedding plans are underway and it's very important that we schedule the cake tasting by next Friday at the latest. If you would please ask her for the date and time, and then call me back tonight or tomorrow, I'd appreciate it." You've asked for specific things, given them a deadline, and been courteous and respectful of the assistant. Provide your cell phone number, your fiancé's cell phone number, and your e-mail address so that they have no excuse for not being able to get in touch with you.

## Keeping the Peace

Phone or in person is the way to go. Some brides and grooms run into trouble when they e-mail the vendor their questions or requests and don't hear anything back. Many of the creative wedding vendors tell me they don't check their e-mail accounts three times a day like other professionals. They might not check them at all, instead leaving that task to their assistants.

What happens when you're still not hearing back? Ask the assistant or the expert for a solution: "Since we're having trouble connecting by phone, please tell me what would work better so that we can partner well on the creation of this cake.

Should we set up a meeting to make all the arrangements, have a tasting, and plan the delivery in one shot?" You've made a concrete request, one the busy cake baker might take you up on.

If there's still no response after repeated attempts, and if going there in person is not an option, take this as proof that you shouldn't depend on this expert to deliver your chosen cake (or any other wedding product or service) in a professional manner. Start the process of removing them from your wedding world. See pages 169–173 for more on firing a vendor.

**Q.** **We'd like our photographer, videographer, and band members to dress more formally to fit in at our wedding. How can we tell them what to wear?**

**A.** They're expecting you to advise them about wardrobe, so a simple, all-business script for you is: "We'd like for you and your assistant to wear tuxedoes to match the style of our wedding. A female assistant should wear a dark-colored dress or suit." It's as simple as that. These experts will be in and among your guests, so it's your right to instruct them on how to dress. Do the same with your limousine or classic car drivers. They, too, should be dressed for the occasion. You can ask your caterer or banquet manager for a description of what their servers will wear. Nearly 100 percent of the time, you'll hear black pants, white shirt, black tie. A direct request is the best way to go.

**Q.** What do we do if the band or disc jockey isn't playing songs from our request list?

**A.** Approach the entertainers during their first break and follow this script:

**YOU:** "Great job, guys! Everyone's having a great time. We're just wondering when you'll be playing the songs we sent you on our playlist a few weeks ago?"

**BAND LEADER:** "Playlist? We didn't get any playlist."

Don't get angry. Get him a piece of paper and write down your song choices—along with your "Do Not Play" list right there in the moment. Don't be shy.

**YOU:** "No problem. The little things can slip through the cracks. So here are the songs we'd love to hear tonight . . . and under no circumstances are you to play the "Chicken Dance," no matter who asks for it. No line dances of any kind, and our crowd loves Motown music. Thank you so much."

You've just stepped in and saved your own reception wishes, and you did so with great diplomacy. It's the passive bride and groom who sit through songs they don't like because they were afraid to say anything.

**Q.** We've heard from friends who flipped out on the wedding day because the food wasn't what they

**expected. If something like this happens, what do we do in the moment?**

**A.** Take your complaints to the caterer in a private location. Ask the caterer or banquet manager to come out into the hallway or into her office, and point out that the scallops you ordered were nowhere to be found, the satay sticks are pork and not chicken, and the pasta bar only has two sauces and not three. Do this early, as soon as possible, without drama or excessive emotion. (No doubt, you will be emotional. And the caterer should see that.)

Start by saying: "Would you please start working now to remedy the situation? I'm sure the hotel has access to a stocked kitchen and freezer, and that your staff can whip up the correct versions of what we ordered, or replacement items. It's simply not going to work for our guests to pick on puff pastry appetizers all night. So please do go see what you can arrange, and we'll talk to you in a short while about what we can expect for our guests." Since the mistakes were theirs, it's their responsibility to bring out something that pleases you, but the catering manager won't be motivated well by a big dose of blame.

Don't worry right now about what things will cost. Just focus on getting good food out to your guests. If the caterer comes back at you with an offer that isn't completely pleasing, here's your second script:

"We ordered certain items from you in good faith, trusting you to deliver. We don't know where the miscommunication happened, or why some foods are not here or are not as we asked, and we're not interested in discussing that now. We have to insist that you produce x, y, and z appetizers as soon as humanly possible. If you can't get these items, then bring out more of what you do have. We're not going to have insufficient food for our guests, so if someone has to go out to the market to buy chicken, then that's what's going to have to happen. This is our wedding, and we know that you're going to do everything in your power to get as close to our original order as possible. We'll sit down and talk about the business end later, but right now, we're expecting you to put your team on this as a matter of the highest priority."

## Keeping the Peace

Problems in the moment are best solved with calmness, good diplomacy, and keeping the vendor accountable in-person. You'll handle this and any other wedding surprises in much the same way.

The caterer doesn't need to be threatened with a lawsuit. You've just said, with class, that you'll talk about all that later.

And it works best to have you, the bride and groom, talk to the caterer with whom you've worked. This conversation will be brief, and you'll feel better about being there and being involved than you would if a bridesmaid or a parent said they'd take care of it for you. Their impulse may be to protect you from the business end, but vendors react better to bride and groom in full wedding-day regalia than they do to an angry bridesmaid or tearful mother. So be direct, state what you expect, and look that vendor in the eye.

**Q.** We need to change our wedding time and some other details, and the first vendor I called about it gave me attitude. Is there a better way to get our vendors to adjust?

**A.** A change in schedule could throw off a busy wedding vendor. If he expected your reception to start at 8 p.m. and now you're saying 4 p.m., that means he has to shuffle his preparation times, his assistants' schedules, his travel time, and any number of other factors. So if you hear attitude, it might just be a natural, human level of overwhelm or the last straw on a very busy day. So don't take the attitude personally.

Just say: "I know this creates a bit of extra work for you, and we appreciate your efforts in making it work." That statement shows that you have empathy for what this change entails for them—many wedding experts say they rarely get such understanding from clients, so they appreciate it all the more.

If your other wedding vendors seem flustered, just accept it as the same kind of initial reaction that you might have if asked to produce a work report five hours earlier than expected. If you'd like a better way to get your vendors to adjust, there really isn't any way you can control their reactions. You can make this as easy as possible with your diplomatic announcement of the change; don't preface it with anything like "you're going to kill us for doing this to you, but we're changing the time." Be positive, don't be overly apologetic (once is fine) since that's not a good motivator, be willing to pay extra for the legwork they may have to do and possibly for hiring more assistants, and thank them for their efforts.

**Q.** The wedding coordinator is on my mother's side! Anything she suggests, the coordinator puts into motion, and they're both telling me my ideas are "off." They're very similar in style, and I'm different from them—but they should be working to create my wedding.

**A.** The two-on-one gang-up is never a fun place to be, especially when it's your wedding that's at stake. When the coordinator clicks with your mother, that's a natural chemistry thing that you're better off accepting; don't try to get the coordinator to click better with you. That's not going to happen, and if you devolve into a mindset of competition, you will lose your focus on the details of your wedding. So let them be best buddies, and invite them for a group meeting where you will remind them both that your shared goal is the success of the wedding plans. Here's your conversation diplomacy script:

> **YOU:** "While it makes me very happy that you enjoy working with one another, I'm feeling that some of my requests are slipping through the cracks. So let's go through some of the plans for the wedding so that I can

fine-tune the details to something more along the lines of what [fiancé] and I want."

You have just established yourself very properly as the main client. Even if Mom is paying, you're the bride. Calling a meeting and setting the agenda shows tremendous self-value.

**MOM:** "Why are you being so difficult? (To the coordinator): "She's always been so difficult." (To you): "Honey, we've already done the reception décor, and we don't want to waste the coordinator's time."

**YOU:** "I'm sure the coordinator would agree that making the bride happy is not a waste of her time, so let's get into this and it will go quickly and smoothly."

**COORDINATOR:** (understanding what's going on here) "Okay, it seems that we've strayed from [bride's] vision for the wedding, so let's go through everything that needs to be tweaked."

There's no need to even approach the incendiary topic that they're a duo and you're on the outside. That doesn't matter to you (or at least that's the image you're projecting to them).

**YOU:** "I don't know if it's struck you this way as we've been working, but you've told me that some of my ideas are a little 'off,' and I don't agree. These are the things that my fiancé and I want, so let's work to make them happen. I'd love to hear your ideas on how we can make them even better, but they're nonnegotiable for us."

The coordinator is going to wish you were her daughter. You're being so respectful, giving them the benefit of the doubt, avoiding blame, and heading right for solutions. And you're honoring the coordinator's expertise.

**MOM:** "Well, there are some things that I want *my* way. . . ."

**YOU:** "We'll take that into account, Mom. I know you're invested in our wedding, and I know certain things are important to you. So when we get to the cake and the entertainment, the things I know you feel strongest about, feel free to share your ideas, and I'm sure we'll be able to get many of them in."

You've thanked her, and you opened the doors for her input. But you've returned yourself to the top of the planning hierarchy.

**Q.** We've noticed that our caterer is tacking on extra charges we didn't agree to.

**A.** Good diplomacy means handling your anger, and this is definitely a situation that can make you angry. While you may want to call up the caterer and yell at him, accusing him of trying to rip you off, that's not the best approach. It could be that an assistant hit a few wrong computer keys and

164

added some charges to your account that were supposed to go to someone else's. I know it's hard to keep this kind of calm perspective when you're stressed and angry, but take a few breaths before you make the call.

"[Caterer]? This is [your name]. I just noticed that a few charges have been added to our bill, and they don't match up to our records. We didn't order a groom's cake, and these cake-cutting charges on this bill don't match the itemized charges on your contract. So I'd like to meet with you and talk about getting these things removed from our bill as soon as possible. When would you have time to meet? Or can we do this over the phone?"

Your caterer may want to review your records, so give him some time to compare the documents. Here's where you might get a surprise: A parent may have called in a change to your order. It happens. Your smart move in calling him allows you to return your order to the original form, get the extra charges removed, and get you all back to working well together.

If the vendor is shady, he or she may argue with you about added charges, saying they told you about them at your first meeting. At this point, I'm sure you're imagining yourself standing up on *The People's Court* and suing the guy for the cost of a groom's cake and cake-cutting fees. It doesn't have to get to that point.

Just say: "You didn't say anything about cake-cutting fees at our first meeting, and we never ordered a groom's cake. We have the original contract here, which also says nothing about those things. So when can I come in to get these charges removed and initialed by you?"

A smart consumer gets everything in writing, and a good diplomat doesn't allow herself to get talked in circles by someone who has a lot of experience swindling brides and grooms to the tune of a whopping $150. If he still argues, use this wording:

"It seems we have some confusion here, so [fiancé] and I will come in to your office to speak with you about it, and if we still can't clear it up, we'll be speaking with your bosses and showing them our original contract." It will amaze you how quickly your caterer will reverse those charges.

## Keeping the Peace

Always get any changes signed and initialed by a wedding vendor. Never leave anything to a verbal agreement. That makes things way harder in court, if it gets to that point.

**Q.** Our wedding vendors are calling my parents—since they're paying—instead of us, for some of the details.

**A.** The wedding vendor has the wrong idea about who the main client is, and needs to be corrected with diplomacy. First of all, this isn't something you need to complain about to your parents, as that's not going to solve the problem. It's not something for them to fix. Call the vendors with this script:

"While my parents are paying for the wedding, the way our planning team works is that you'll call me and my fiancé with all information about the wedding, any questions or concerns, and anything else we have to arrange." That's it. No whining about how the vendors are cutting you out of the planning, how upsetting it is to get calls from your mother about the menu and you haven't even seen it yet. That may be true, but it's not part of your best diplomacy. When you're pleasant and direct about it, the vendors will be only too happy to make the change on their records, take down all of your phone numbers and e-mail addresses, and the contact chain takes the form it should have had in the first place. At this point, you can let your parents know that you've spoken to the vendors .

**YOU:** "It's just much easier on us, and then you don't have to be the middleman. Whatever we find out, we'll share with you." You're not asking, you're informing.

**PARENTS:** "You're firing us? After all we've done for this wedding? That's the most ungrateful thing. . . ."

**YOU:** "This has nothing to do with the great job you're doing for our wedding, which we really appreciate and count ourselves very lucky to have. It's just that we prefer to speak directly to the vendors so that we can correct any mistakes and get things done more efficiently." Then remind your parents how happy you are to share the wedding plans with them. "We appreciate your generosity and understanding." Key phrase.

**Q.** We asked for a funny theme cake for our reception and our baker doesn't want to do it. We love her work and her prices, so how can we convince her to do this one theme cake?

**A.** You can't. If your cake baker—or any wedding vendor you ask to create a specialty item or service—doesn't want to do it, they're not going to do it. If you love her work, perhaps you can have her design a traditional, smaller cake for your reception, and then get another baker to create that funny theme cake as your groom's cake, or even the cake for your rehearsal dinner. If that's too much extra cake, then find a different cake baker to design and make the cute, funny cake you want.

**Q.** We don't like the samples our florist sent us. And this is her second attempt. How can we tell her to try again without seeming demanding?

**A.** Don't worry about seeming demanding. As the bride and groom, investing so much in a very special celebration, you can be demanding. Your point of diplomacy here is to communicate with friendly respect to your florist to guide her course and still keep her on a relationship level where she wants to make you happy. "You're not getting it" will put her on the defensive, insult her, and make her far less likely to be invested in you or your wedding. This is better:

"We looked at your newest samples, and they're getting closer to what we have in mind." You're providing positive reinforcement. "How about we come in with some additional pictures for you, and we can talk in further depth about exactly what we'd like for our wedding? What works best with your schedule?" You're solution-oriented, and a good professional will not take any offense at how you've described what you want. You're working to make her job easier, too. I'm sure she's frustrated at not being able to capture what you want, since wedding experts pride themselves at reading their clients well and delivering well.

**Q.** **We need to fire our wedding coordinator. We know we have to do it in writing, but how can we do this in a diplomatic way? Many of our vendors came through her referral.**

**A.** It's never easy to fire a wedding coordinator—or any other wedding vendor—so apply this advice to all of your experts. When you have an irreconcilable problem with a vendor, sometimes the only recourse is to cut ties. Your wedding is too important to keep an irresponsible or unresponsive professional on your team. Whatever the reason for your dissatisfaction with the expert, you'll need to be able to express it both verbally and in writing to the expert as a matter of legality and decency.

Legally, your contract probably has a cancellation clause. In those terms, you've been instructed on how to cancel your association with the expert in a way and with timing that allows you at least a partial refund. Some experts say that you can have 100 percent of your deposit returned, and owe no more, if you notify the vendor in writing by a certain date. If you cancel within six months of the wedding, you may only get 50 percent back (since the time the vendor spent on your wedding plans took away from her time with others' weddings). Some contracts say you don't get any deposit back if you cancel. Look at your contract and find the cancellation terms, and then you can work on your diplomatic plan to fire your vendor.

Since she did refer you to many of your additional experts, you may feel that you'd like to stay on her good side, and especially if there is no conflict—you just can't afford her now that your budget has become more realistic—you'll want to be decent about your next steps. And even if you had a horrible experience with a vendor, it's still better for you to take the high road and be professional in whatever you say and write to cancel your partnership.

That said, here's your script for firing a vendor by phone:

"[Vendor's name], I'm calling to let you know that we've decided to terminate our contract with you."

Keep it professional. If you've had ongoing problems with the vendor, tried everything to resolve them, and still couldn't come to agreement or satisfaction, you'll say:

"We've tried several ways to resolve our creative differences over the wedding, and we just don't see our working styles blending in the way we'd like them to."

Don't say, "we don't like your working style" or "you haven't given us the time of day." The vendor might be stunned, and she might want to entice you back into working with her. After all, word-of-mouth referrals are essential to any wedding professional, and she might worry that you'll speak badly of her work. And it does hurt a professional's pride when a client wants to walk. For some professionals, this call is a shocker if they didn't know the client was unhappy in the first place.

**VENDOR:** "Why don't we sit down and talk about this? I wasn't aware that you had such big concerns."

The decision is yours at this point. If you do like the vendor, and you admit you haven't been completely honest about your feelings with her, and there is a chance that you can solve your differences, go in for the meeting. If you're sure this is what you want to do, then you'll follow that offer with:

**YOU:** "No, we've talked about this at length. It wasn't an easy decision, but it's what we'd like to do. Thank you for the time and effort you spent on working with us thus far, and we'll send you a written confirmation of our cancellation so that we can get our deposit back."

You're strong yet polite in your wording, and you've set down the process of how things will go from here. Resist the urge to get into further details, as your emotions can kick in. This is, after all, not a pleasant thing for either of you to deal with. And some brides and grooms slip into a litany of complaints that give a vendor a chance to lure you back in. And it's just not necessary to go into details that don't serve your goals: "My mother said you were rude to her" isn't a topic that can be solved, and it gets you off course. So stick with your statement, express gratitude for even the smallest efforts on your expert's part, and get right into the cancellation process, which requires written confirmation of your cancellation.

The written confirmation is simply a brief letter—not an e-mail—written to the expert stating that you're terminating the working relationship and why (write specifically why; avoid vague wording, like "Inability to meet with us in a timely manner, creative differences, etc."). It's the document that states and supports your request for a refund of your deposit, and also protects you from owing further money. It should be written in a polite style, closing with thanking the vendor for her time and referrals.

Then follow up with a separate, brief e-mail of thanks when the process is underway or completed.

**Q.** We need to fire a wedding vendor with whom we have no other ties. Is it okay to just send a letter, or do we have to talk with him?

**A.** Yes, you do need to make personal contact in addition to sending a letter. After all, a letter can get lost in the mail. Without personal contact, you might assume she got the letter, and then by the time you hear differently, you're already in the sixty-days-or-less time frame in which refunds are not possible. When you call, here's your script:

"[Vendor's name], thank you for all of your work on our wedding, but we've decided to end our partnership with you. We feel our working styles are too different, and we can't see that changing. So we'll send an official letter of notification, and we'd like a letter of confirmation from you. Again, thanks for your time, and we wish you all the best."

If the vendor protests, wanting as any caring professional would to keep your business, your friendly let-down is direct:

"Thank you, but no. We talked about this for a while, and it's our final decision. Again, we wish you all the best." When you hang up, you'll feel good about yourself for being so strong, so decent, so respectful, and so direct.

**Q.** We interviewed several bakers, but the one we hired has just told us that she can't do our cake. How do we go back to a baker that we chose not to hire and say that we'd now like to work with him?

**A.** Don't worry about the baker thinking he's your second choice. He probably doesn't even remember you if it's been a while. Rather than apologize or go to him sheepishly, approach your new vendor with a fresh start.

Say: "[Vendor's name], we'd love to meet with you about our wedding cake."

If he does remember you and makes any comment about how you originally turned him down, here's your best wording: "In all the wedding planning craziness, we made a few choices that we're now correcting. We love your work and hope that we can have your cake at our reception."

The vendor is a professional, and you're a paying client. It's time now to get into the details. Apologies are not necessary, so don't worry yourself about any vendor's hurt feelings. That's most often not the case.

**Q.** Our caterer recommended a cake baker with whom he works often, but we've decided to hire a different baker. What should we say to the caterer when he finds out we didn't use his referral?

**A.** Your caterer—like any wedding vendor—isn't likely to take it personally if you don't use his referrals, since you're free to hire whomever you'd like. If he does mention it, just say, "Thanks for your referral, but we found one who makes the style of cake we want." Keep it short and simple, since no explanation is needed. Then move on to your discussions about the catering.

Chapter 6

# Guests Behaving Badly

Sometimes they don't mean any harm, but guests can cause problems for you when they have expectations about your wedding, or if they simply say the wrong thing at the wrong moment. Since these are your family, friends, colleagues, and future in-laws, whatever they do presents you with an opportunity to solve the problem diplomatically. I say opportunity because guest diplomacy has a ripple effect. Guests do talk with one another, as in one aunt calling the other aunt to ask if an invitation arrived or when the shower is, so when you handle that first aunt's question with skillful tact and poise, the news gets to the second aunt and goes onward.

Keep in mind, again, that when you're dealing with such a large group of people, you'll have a large group of opinions. Some people believe in old-world etiquette and expect you to do things by the book, while others are far more understanding of today's necessary bending of etiquette. Some have certain expectations based on your relationship to them. Weddings bring out some pretty surprising reactions and requests from people, and again not all of them are intentionally hurtful. So be careful to stick with the topic at hand and not fuel a larger problem by getting emotional or reading meanings that aren't there.

## Keeping the Peace

As a matter of good diplomacy, keep your anger in check and find a safe place to vent, like a journal or through exercise. Remember that relationships exist after the wedding, and you'll want to handle all of these relationships with care now.

With many of your guest issues, there's another element that comes into play: You're going to get outside input and influence from your parents, friends, and others. There's going to be a significant amount of pressure to be fair to people, and all of your advisers will think that they know the best way to handle each problem that comes up. It's going to be tempting to chat about these problems with others, or even complain about these problems with others, but that, too, has a ripple effect. In a heightened emotional state, you might fire off a complaining e-mail to a friend that spreads the story around.

After you've solved the problem in a clear state, you've done irreversible damage to a friendship and to your reputation as a kindhearted, gracious person.

**Q.** Several of our long-distance relatives have written us about the wedding, and we weren't planning on inviting them due to space and budget limits. How can we break the news to them?

**A.** This is one that can be tempting to run away from, just say nothing, and know they'll get the picture when the invitation never shows up. The path of least resistance. But you're better than that. When relatives contact you with questions about the wedding, here's your script:

> **YOU:** "We wish we could invite all of our relatives, but we've run into space and budget problems. So we had to draw the line at first cousins." Or that the site you wanted only has space for 100 people. "[Your fiancé's name] has an enormous family," is fine to share, if that's true. It won't do to blame your intended and then have your invited relatives report that he only had twenty people from his side at the wedding. Your family loves you and will very likely understand your need to keep your guest list small, especially if other weddings in your family have been guest-limited too.

**RELATIVE:** "Oh, we were so looking forward to seeing everyone! You know, with everyone living so far apart now, we only get together for weddings and funerals these days." Nice guilt trip, Auntie.

**YOU:** "Well, we have the family Christmas party coming up in a few months, and the family reunion next summer. So we'll all be together at those events, which are going to be a lot of fun."

Aunt Guilt Trip hasn't wangled an invitation to the wedding, and you have shown your dedication to the family and excitement about future events.

Now, if the relative offers to send a gift anyway, you can say the expected "no, you don't have to," but if your relative insists and is so good at heart as to offer you a present, just say thank you.

**Q.** A lot of our friends are upset that we're planning a destination wedding with just our families and a few of our closest friends. Can we plan a second celebration to share with them?

**A.** Absolutely. Post–destination wedding celebrations are a huge trend right now, and they range from big, informal barbecues to big, formal dinners. Anything you'd like. So handle the issue very diplomatically right now by mailing out pretty save the date cards to everyone on your invitation list.

Your save the date card would call the event "a celebration of our marriage," which makes it clear to guests that this isn't the wedding. You can also add to your save the date card, or to invitations if you'd like to send them now instead, excited wording to share your news: "We couldn't wait! We got married in Hawaii on [date], and we'd love to celebrate with all of our family and friends. . . ."

**Q.** **We don't have the space and budget to allow our single friends to bring guests to the wedding. But some have been in long-term relationships, and it wouldn't be fair to allow some to bring guests while others aren't allowed.**

**A.** At the time of this writing, tempers are flaring at the *www.PashWeddings.com* Web site where I answer questions—a bride told her friend that she couldn't bring a date to the wedding. She checked with other friends, and they had been given an "and guest." The friend felt singled out (no pun intended), slighted, hurt, and is considering not going to the wedding. And who could blame her? Many people interpret a lack of "and guest" to be extremely rude—from an etiquette standpoint and from a personal standpoint ("You think I can't get a date?" "What? I'm the single one? The loser?")—and then there are those who get lost in the fuzzy definition of "in a relationship."

Some couples, innocently trying to work their guest lists to fit their space and budget constraints, create rules. They'll only give an "and guest" if a couple is engaged or living together, for instance.

Please don't try to sway your guests into not bringing a date if they're not in a serious relationship. It boggles the mind to think that anyone would call a friend and say, "I know I gave you an "and guest," but since you're not seeing anyone seriously, and since we have big guest list issues, would you please not bring a date?" It happens all the time, and people on the receiving end of this gaffe can get offended.

The rules are yours to make, and most guests just accept them. If you do get a call or e-mail in protest about a lack of "and guest," here is your most diplomatic wording:

"We just don't have the space or budget for so many guests, and we want all of our family and closest friends there. So we had to make this tough decision and apply it to everyone, friends and family alike. I'm sorry you're offended, but there's nothing we can do. We can't make exceptions, or this will turn into a nightmare."

You'll be happy to know that most brides and grooms who limited their guest lists like this never heard any complaints from their guests.

**Q.** The reception will be at a five-star hotel, and we know that many of our guests won't be able to afford rooms there. The nearest budget hotel is far away and it's not too nice.

**A.** It's wonderful of you to consider your guests' needs. Before you worry about the diplomatic way to tell them the only other option is a fleabag motel twenty minutes down the road, check additional options: bed and breakfasts, other nearby hotels, and ask the five-star hotel where your wedding will be held if they can give you a nice discount on rooms for your guests. Ask if they offer AAA or military discounts for guests, student discounts, if they have specials, and so on. Find as many different options as possible, and include a detailed card with your invitation. It's best to provide three different options, listing the price ranges for rooms on each, as well as any discounts you find for them. Guests appreciate seeing this considerate gesture on the card, and then you're removed from any diplomatic needs. The guests will make their own arrangements, and some may even choose to stay with friends in the area or share a room when they see the prices you list.

**Q.** My parents say it's our responsibility to pay the travel and lodging expenses of our guests, and we've read that is no longer the case.

**A.** You're right. That is no longer the case. Some couples and their families do offer to pay for travel and lodging for special guests, and some do have the budget to pay for everyone's expenses—but that is a matter of personal choice and ability. Just tell your parents that wedding experts say this is no longer an obligation.

**Q.** It's three weeks until our wedding and some of our guests haven't RSVP'd.

**A.** You don't want to be pushy, but it's not like you're demanding an answer a month before the RSVP date. So, either tackle this one yourselves or ask a parent, maid of honor, or best man to help out by making calls to these people with a simple and friendly, "We're just finalizing our guest list headcount for the caterer, and we'd like to know if you will be coming to the wedding." Short, simple, to the point. No attitude or comment about them not bothering to respond by the RSVP date like all of the responsible people you know. Sarcasm isn't a part of good diplomacy, so stick to your objective: getting an answer. You might find out that they did mail back their response card weeks ago, but it never reached you.

**Q.** We sent out our Save the Dates almost a year in advance, and some of our guests thought that was the invitation—even though it said "invitation to follow." They're calling with tons of questions about the hotel, and calling us "unorganized." How can we deal with these people?

**A.** Save the Date cards are relatively new in the wedding world, and some of your relatives obviously don't know what they are. So here's your perfect response, whether you have to deliver it over the phone or through e-mail: "That was just the Save the Date card, which we sent out to make sure that our wedding wouldn't conflict with your potential vacation plans, and so that you'd have plenty of time to make your travel arrangements. In a week or so, we'll have our personalized wedding Web site up with all of the hotel and wedding information, so I'll contact you then to make sure you get all the details you need. I'm really looking forward to seeing you at the wedding." Your friendly demeanor disarms the person who's just looking to criticize your actions, and the confused get the information they need. You'll get all kinds of reactions to every step you take, so keep your diplomacy by giving everyone the benefit of the doubt, showing how your Save the Dates were an act of consideration for them, and assuring them that they'll get the details they're so anxious for. And then, of course, follow through on your offer. Make a note to call or e-mail when you do have the details posted on your site, which you may have to explain to guests who have never seen one of those either. Especially with grandparents and older guests, it's possible that Internet wedding planning tools are a mystery.

**Q.** One of our guests won't commit to attend the wedding. She keeps saying, "I'll have to see what my work schedule is."

**A.** Call her or send her an e-mail saying, "We'd love to know if you'll be coming to the wedding. Our deadline for giving the caterer our final headcount is Friday, so we have to know before then. Just give me a call or shoot me an e-mail either way. Thanks."

Don't waste your time trying to figure out why she's stalling. Problems arise from assumptions. So take her word that it's her unpredictable work schedule and focus on the only fact that matters: whether or not she and her guest will attend. If she still doesn't respond by Friday, now it's time to check on her. Give her a call to say hello, ask what's going on in her world, and you may get the answer that allows you to be a good friend. She might be depressed, overworked, caring for a sick parent, or going through a tough time. Encourage her to come to the wedding if she'd like, but if this stall has been from fear of saying no to you, then your script is:

"[Friend's name], don't worry at all. I completely understand that you're going through a tough time right now, and even though we'll miss you at the wedding, we know you have to do what's best for your family (for you, for school, for the kids, etc.). We'll be sure to get together with you after the wedding." Or, maybe she'd like to get together for coffee and a chat very soon. Busy brides sometimes get tunnel vision and forget that guests have complicated lives of their own. This kind of stalling can be a symptom of that, but, again, you don't know the facts until you talk with her.

**Q.** A friend of mine wants to bring her boyfriend, who is a big loser. He always gets drunk and sloppy at other weddings and we'd rather not have him there.

**A.** If you tell your friend that she can't bring her boy-friend to your wedding, your relationship will be strained, if not severed. Sure, you can see that the guy acts like a loser, but she sees something different. My best advice, looking at diplomacy only, is not to say anything. If he acts up at your wedding, tell your friend that you're very unhappy about his behavior, you don't want him disrupting your wedding (don't say "ruin," since that's giving him too much credit), and say, "I'd like for you to take him out of here, please." Confront the friend, not the drunk guy. If you would prefer, your parent or other authority figure can talk to your friend in your place while you continue to enjoy your party. Prepare for the pos-sibility of an outburst from him by getting several members of the bridal party to stand nearby in case backup is needed. Another pre-planned step, as mentioned earlier in this book: talk to the site manager or wedding coordinator about what they should do to remove disruptive guests. Chances are very good that they see this kind of thing every weekend, so they might already have half a dozen staff members to take care of this with one request from you.

**Q.** We've created a backup guest list in case our top-tier guests can't come, but it's going to be obvi-ous when the invitations show up late.

**A.** If anyone suspects this scenario, they'll likely keep it to themselves. Here's your script if you hear one of the most common responses:

**SARCASTIC GUEST:** "Oh, so you invited us after everyone else said no?" Laugh it off with the following:

**YOU:** "It simply took us a while to get your envelope addressed."

It's not an answer to their statement, and it is true. They're being the troublemaker with the comment, and you've just deflected it with smart diplomacy.

## Keeping the Peace

Some things do not need to be discussed, which is also a key to good diplomacy.

**Q.** I'm getting a lot of pressure to invite friends I haven't spoken to in a long time. Our other friends would be angry if we didn't, and they said they wouldn't come if we leave the others out.

**A.** Wow, that's very manipulative of them. Group dynamics like this present big challenges for those who wish to be diplomatic and respectful of others (something these friends seem to have a little trouble with). So here's your diplomatic wording for the friends you did invite:

"I wish we could invite them, but we both had to make some very tough choices as we made our final guest list. We only have room for 100, so we had to draw the line at friends with whom we're in regular and close contact. It wasn't easy for us, and while we know you're just looking out for [uninvited friends], we hope you'll still be able to come to the wedding. We'll have to plan something to get together with all of our friends after the wedding, but for right now, there are a bunch of people we wish we could invite but can't."

Of course, you might look at this problem as an opportunity to get back in touch with the distant friends, and not even think about how it would seem that you did so only after your friends' threat. Let that slide, as it's really not important.

**Q.** Some of our relatives offered to help make our invitations and favors, but they haven't delivered and they haven't answered my e-mails or calls about them.

**A.** Let them off the hook. Not returning repeated attempts to contact them means they aren't on top of the task, so speak with them in a way that makes you the hero in offering a gracious way out. Here's your script:

**YOU:** "I know it was a long time ago when you offered to make the favors, and I know that things have gotten quite busy for you since the kids started school (or since the semester started, or since the holidays are approaching—whatever works). So it's completely understandable if you'd rather not take this on right now. I'm happy to take care of it, since everything is planned and (laugh) I'm a little bit bored right now."

**RELATIVE:** "Oh, no. That's not necessary. Besides, I don't want to break my word." (Even though you just gave them permission to.) You have two options now. If the situation is one of unfortunate delay, you might hear this:

**RELATIVE:** "I can make the favors. I've just been waiting for supplies to be shipped, and they should be in on Thursday."

**YOU:** "That's terrific! But since the wedding is coming up so quickly, how about I either help you or find you an assistant, someone who can help make them and make the labels?" Sometimes, good-natured people sign on to help, but they find out later that the task is way more involved than expected. Your offer to help or find a volunteer might be very welcome news that still allows them to save face.

If this volunteer still wants to make the items without any help, here's your script:

**YOU:** "Great. I'm sure they're going to be lovely. I do have to give you a firm deadline of October 1, though, since that's when we'd like to have all of our supplies in order. Does that give you enough time?" Make that deadline way ahead of the wedding so that you can buy or make replacements if you have to. Finish up with, "Call me if you have any questions about the design or anything at all." And then call again a week before the deadline just to ask how things are coming along:

**YOU:** "Just checking in to see how the favors are coming along, if there's anything you need or anything I can do to help out."

Does that make you a pest? Maybe, depending on the mood the person is in when you call. But you'd be a smart pest to stay on top of things.

**Q.** We won't be inviting all of our guests to the rehearsal dinner, as it would be like a second wedding celebration, so we'd like to let them know where they can go for dinner or drinks (but not on us).

**A.** Just send them a pre-wedding note—printed on your computer or e-mailed is fine—with a friendly greeting, along with "We wanted you to know about our favorite restaurants in the area, for your Friday night plans. We hope you'll all have fun getting together with friends and family you haven't seen in a while! Here are the restaurants: [and then provide the name, street address, Web site, and a brief description of the food style—Brazilian, Japanese, Italian, etc.]." Some couples make this diplomatic note extra-fun by sharing little stories about each place: "This is where we had our first date!" and "Try the crème brûlée—it's amazing!" You've looked out for your guests and made it clear that it's on them.

**Q.** A few relatives have insisted that we provide them with vegan meals, and that's not something we arranged with our caterer. How can we tell them it's not their place to tell us what to have on the menu?

**A.** Instead of taking a stand on your relatives' request, and whether or not it was appropriate for them to tell you what to have on the menu, contact your caterer about seeing if any of your existing choices meet vegan standards, and if you can still order three vegan meals. As the party's hosts, you're more correct in making the special request for the menu, and meeting your guests' needs if the request is easy to fill. You don't want to get embroiled in a big custom-order scenario where you're calling constantly with special requests for food allergies, kosher meals, vegetarian entrées, and kids' meals with allergy requirements. So take each request as it comes, and tell guests the following:

"We'll try to accommodate your request, but the order is already in with the caterer. There will be plenty of vegan/vegetarian/organic/peanut-free options through the cocktail party and the dinner." (If that's true, of course.) "I'll get back to you with the caterer's answer on this." And do so.

It's up to you if you'd like to change one of your entrées or courses to fit a vegetarian or kosher requirement, or add a new course or entrée, when you know that many of your guests will want the same option.

**Q.** We've decided not to have alcohol at our reception due to our religious beliefs, and we know this is going to be a big problem for many of our guests.

**A.** If guests have a problem with your decision not to have alcohol, they actually have a much larger problem than is your responsibility to solve. Stick to your guns, don't be pressured to cross your own deep religious values to make others happy, and know that these people will find alcohol at another location shortly after your wedding. If you find yourself in a position of being asked about it, you need go no further than this script:

"We've made a decision according to our religious beliefs, as well as the rules of the reception site," like a church hall, "not to have alcohol at our reception. But since we know that many of our guests will want to celebrate with drinks, we'll let everyone know some great clubs or lounges where they can gather after the wedding."

**Q.** Several guests didn't show up at our wedding. I'm angry, and my mother is concerned about them. How do I approach them about this?

**A.** The two reactions (anger and concern) are completely understandable in this situation, so your most diplomatic move is to go with the latter. Obviously, something happened to prevent them from coming, so before your hurt feelings lead you into anger and insult, take that breath and consider that maybe your guest was sick, had a sick child, received devastating news, had an emergency in the family, and so on. So call the guests who didn't show with nothing more than concern for them.

Try saying: "We missed you at the wedding, and I'm just calling to make sure that everything is okay. Call me back as soon as you can." Resist the urge to check in with the gossip mill, because that group is the enemy of diplomacy. When you reach the people who didn't show, they'll give you a reason they missed the wedding, and probably will apologize for not calling you. There may be some shrinking from responsibility, but that's a matter of their integrity and character. "I didn't want to upset you before the wedding," could very well be the truth, if the news of a relative's grave illness was the reason for the no-show. The family wasn't ready to share the news, and they didn't want to cast a pall over your day. They had no options. So release them from your anger and be a good friend or relative with an offer to help in any way you can.

When the reason is not one worthy of empathy, such as "I wrote down the wrong day," or "I forgot," or "I didn't want to face my ex-husband," your annoyance is certainly understandable here.

In this situation, saying: "We really wish you would have called," in a curt and direct tone is completely fine. No need to launch into how much money you wasted on them or what each guest's dinner cost, as that makes it seem like you want them to pay you back. While that sounds fair, it's really not a demand you can make in good diplomacy. Yes, they wasted your money, and they caused you and your family unnecessary concern. That's something to keep in mind for the relationship you'll have with them in the future. Now I'm not suggesting that you go for revenge and not show up to their wedding when you responded that you would. It's just a chance for you to assess how much you'll trust and invest in them in the future.

**Q.** Lots of guests have said that they can't make it to the ceremony, but they'll be at the reception. That's incredibly rude! And our photos will show a sparse crowd at the ceremony.

**A.** This trend has grown, unfortunately, and it's quite sad. Some guests say it's to save them money on babysitters, or give them more travel time on the day of the wedding. Whatever the reason, some guests see no problem in skipping the ceremony—the most important part of your wedding day—and showing up just for the reception. Unfortunately, there's no way that you can tell guests they have to attend the ceremony. If you're concerned about your photos, talk with your photographer about your wish to have him expertly style the photos so that no evidence exists of low attendance. That's how they make movies as well—they fill one section of a stadium with people, shoot that, and then fill in with different full-stadium shots later. If you'd like, arrange with your photographer to plan a full guest list group photo at the start of the reception. Some couples lead all of their guests outside into the garden where the photographer beautifully captures the kind of all-inclusive shot you want.

**Q.** I'd like to invite my work friends to the wedding, but not everyone I work with. That's going to cause major drama at the office.

**A.** Diplomacy in the office is a subject unto itself. Getting along with coworkers in a very status-charged atmosphere takes almost constant diplomacy and emotional maturity every day, so when you add the topic of your wedding to the social and professional dynamics of your workplace, things can get pretty sticky. Most people have a core group of work friends and close colleagues. They're the ones you lunch with, socialize with, invite to cocktail parties at your house, and the ones you've probably spent at-work hours talking to about your wedding. These people would, of course, be invited to the wedding. I'm sure that's not your problem.

It gets dicey when those satellite coworkers sniff out your wedding and want to be included, want to belong. And those satellite people could include a manager or some other person who is influential in your career status, assignments, responsibilities, and upward mobility at the office. The problem is, they're not on your A-list. It's a judgment call on your part. More people are including extended work groups in their wedding guest lists, since it's these people with whom they spend the majority of their time, and it's these people who can have an influence on their careers. It's almost a "must" invite. Again, it's your choice, and many couples do add them to their lists. It couldn't hurt if there's room, after all.

But what about the extended acquaintances, those who have heard about your wedding, know you only from office hours, and—just like in high school—seem to think they're a closer friend to you than they really are? It gets tricky there, since these people could be the ones who create drama if they aren't invited. At least, that's the fear of many brides and grooms.

As a matter of diplomacy, you'll define the clear, dark edges of your inner circle by the sending of your wedding invitations. Word will get around, and when the satellite people approach you with hurt and confusion about being left out, your answer carries a professional diplomacy:

"We only had so much space," and leave out the budget part, "and we both come from large families. So we only had a finite number of spaces available for our work friends and associates after we included our longtime closest friends," and leave out the word acquaintances for its loaded impression. "We wish we could have everyone at the office join us, but we had to limit it to just the people we socialize with outside the office." These acquaintances will see that yes, they really haven't socialized with you on a more personal level. Understanding your parameters in a clear way, they will likely fade off from the problem.

**Q.** I'd like to invite my bosses to the wedding, since they've asked about my wedding plans, but doesn't this cross the line?

**A.** No, it doesn't. If your bosses have been aware of your wedding plans, and if you have a positive relationship with them, it's great diplomacy to invite them. The boss loves to be seen as a person, too.

**Q.** I'd rather not invite the family friends and neighbors that were invited to my sister's wedding a few years ago. Can I explain to them that it's a matter of space and money? I feel like I have to include everyone my sister included, and she had a larger budget than I have.

**A.** This one is tough, since you know that all these people will have an expectation of being invited. It may not make sense to them that they'd make the cut for one sister and not for the other. You'll probably get a lot of parental input, which will only ratchet up the pressure factor, so consider your next move carefully. Rather than invite drama and confusion by attempting to explain to guests why you didn't invite them, just send out your invitations to those who have made the cut.

World leaders have said that good diplomacy works even better when you have your allies supporting the same diplomacy. So talk with your parents—who are likely to be the ones to get the questioning calls from the left-out people—to provide them with the best way to handle the inquiries.

Their script: "[Your name] is planning a more intimate wedding," is far better than mentioning you're on a smaller budget. "So the guest list is limited to eighty people, including his side. A larger wedding like [sister's name] is not her style. We're very sorry that we can't share the day with you, but we'll see you at [upcoming event that isn't your wedding.]" Of course, if they call you, that's your script too. Most people are extremely understanding and accommodating, and with a packed schedule they may be relieved not to have another social event to attend. And some may even send gifts as a matter of their own personal diplomacy with family and friends. That's not your goal, of course, but it has been reported as a pleasant surprise by many brides, grooms, and families who handled this problem with friendly and honest responses.

**Q.** Some of our guests are complaining about having to travel so far for our wedding. We got better prices in my fiancé's home state, so it was natural for us to plan it for there. People are calling us "inconsiderate."

**A.** While destination weddings are on the rise, guests aren't quite up on the popularity of it. After all, they may have to take time off of work, pay big amounts for travel and lodging, board their pets, have someone watch their kids for the weekend, have someone watch their house for the weekend, and so on. This is why most couples plan destination weddings with only a handful of guests invited. Their nearest and dearest wouldn't mind paying for the equivalent of a vacation to be there for your day. When you invite 250 people to travel five hours for your wedding, you do obligate them to spend a chunk of money and time for you . . . in addition to what has increasingly become a more generous wedding gift in addition to shower gifts. So it's not a mystery that some guests consider a large, destination wedding to be inconsiderate. Given that they have a valid point according to their perspective, your best diplomacy in this case is to assure them that you'll make it worth their while with an unforgettable wedding weekend.

Just say: "We're planning a cocktail party for everyone the night before the wedding, the resort has four pools and free jet skiing, and the wedding itself is going to be an extravaganza."

Guests who stewed about having to travel so far for your wedding will now have a change of perspective: you've thought of them, you've gotten them free and fun activities, and the entire event sounds more like a wonderful group vacation. That's far from being inconsiderate. Of course, this all hinges on your taking special care to plan special events for guests who travel to the state where the wedding will take place. Sometimes, activities are another form of your diplomacy.

**Q.** Our cousin recently eloped, and they've asked if they can have a spotlight dance at our wedding to get good photos. That's sponging off of our wedding, so what's the best way to say no?

**A.** Some people really have guts, don't they? This is quite a request—"Hey, you're paying $2,000 for your photographer, and every minute of your five-hour wedding reception costs about $300, so we'd like you to pay for us to have our moment in the spotlight!" Money aside, it's quite rude of anyone to ask to use your wedding as their personal big moment. (I do reserve judgment on family members who ask the bride and groom's permission to share happy family news—like an engagement, a pregnancy, or a guest's fiftieth wedding anniversary or birthday—when that genuinely adds to the joy of the event.) These cousins, however, are looking for their own moment of joy, and they're hoping you'll be an easy mark. I know it's tough to say no in the moment, so here's your best response:

"Give me some time to talk with [your fiancé] about this." Then, take some time to think about how you feel about their request—that won't take long!—and then talk with your fiancé and parents about it, if you'd like. When you've stepped away from the situation, you can calm yourself, and then deliver the diplomatic "no" that the situation requires.

"We have a lot of friends who have big moments of their own, many relatives who eloped or have just gotten engaged, and it would open a big can of worms if we started giving out spotlight dances to one couple," is a great way to start. Remind them to think about your relationships with others. "Plus, this really is our special day, and we just don't feel comfortable with your request. So why don't you just ask a relative to take some photos of you dancing at our wedding. We'll gladly play your song—as long as it's not the same as ours—but it won't be a spotlight dance." You've shown that you thought it out, and you worked to find a good solution for them that works for you too. If they get offended, that's their character on display. And let your bandleader know that no one is to request a spotlight dance for themselves during your reception. Disc jockeys and bandleaders are on to this ploy, so they'll be able to diplomatically turn down any stealth requests.

**Q.** We have some relatives who don't get along, and we're going to need good diplomacy rules about the seating arrangements.

**A.** This is more strategy than diplomacy. Place these people at distant tables, and split up their circle of friends so that they can each sit with people they know. It wouldn't be good diplomacy, or good strategy, to seat one of the warring parties with complete strangers. Building a seating chart can be a tricky task, but with a good amount of time devoted to switching tables and mixing up your side with his side—who says all tables have to be his side and her side?—you'll build seating arrangements with all the talent and skill of White House social secretaries.

## Keeping the Peace

The guests are seated according to common interests or existing relationships, ensuring that each group will have a great time together.

**Q.** Our parents have invited a lot of extra people without checking with us. How can we un-invite them?

**A.** Your parents got a little overexcited and acted on their assumptions. Now that your wedding plans are underway and your guest list set, the guests your parents invited will need to be informed that they won't make the list. It's not good form to get the message across by just not sending an invitation to each of them. The good news is that this diplomacy solution falls to your parents. They did the inviting, and now they need to undo the invitations to their friends and hoped-for guests. Have empathy for them, as this is not an easy thing to do. If your parents, who will understandably be a little nervous and upset about their mistake, their embarrassment, and not wanting to hurt their friends' feelings, offer to pay for their extra guests, then the problem might be solved that way.

201

But if there's no room, and if your budget is stretched, they do have to make the tough calls.

Your good diplomacy here is asking your parents to do this the right way: "Mom, Dad, we'd like you to take care of calling your book club friends and your country club friends to let them know that we can't invite them to the wedding." Before your parents even get a chance to spin out an argument or a distraction, offer this: "I read a book on wedding diplomacy, and here's the best way to say it right, without hurting anyone's feelings." That should get them to listen. Tell them to use this script:

"The wedding plans are underway, and it turns out that my excitement got ahead of me. While we would love to have you at the wedding, the guest list of closest family and friends turned out much larger than expected. So I'm very sorry that I invited you before the plans were finalized, and I have to let you know that we won't be able to ask you to join us. It's simply a matter of space and budget, a large guest list on the groom's side, and the site the kids picked is a bit smaller than I expected. I hope you understand." Good friends will appreciate getting a full, genuine, and considerate expression of value in the relationship and an explanation of the very understandable limits to your wedding guest list.

**Q.** My aunt wants us to hire her friend to do our invitations, but we don't like the samples we've seen.

**A.** Helpful and good-hearted relatives and friends will likely offer to help with your wedding plans, to share in the excitement, and help you get the wedding of your dreams personalized without costing you a fortune. To turn down this well-meaning loved one, just follow this script:

"While we so appreciate your efforts to help us get great invitations from your friend, we found a terrific invitation shop we've fallen in love with, and we're going to get our print items from them. But thank you so much for all the time and energy you put into connecting us, and if we ever hear of anyone who wants invitations of this style, we'll pass along your friend's contact information." Done. No need to talk about how you didn't like the style. That's not important. Your goal is not to judge the talent, but to thank your aunt for her help and get yourselves into the freedom to order your own invitations.

**Q.** I'm losing weight to fit into my bridal gown, and people are being obnoxious about it, saying that I'm only losing weight so that I'll look good on the wedding day, but that I'll "balloon up again" afterward. I'm a healthy size 8, I feel terrific, and it's really upsetting me that people are saying I'm starving myself.

**A.** Isn't it amazing that people will jump right to a negative assumption? Without analyzing them too much, or trying to find any ulterior motive in their comments (um, sabotage?), your best diplomacy lies in a response like this: "Yes, my trainer and I have been working very hard, and my fiancé and I have taken up basketball. So getting in shape for the wedding has turned into a healthier lifestyle for both of us." Use the word "healthier," since getting healthy is certainly what you're doing. There's no need to defend yourself too much, as getting defensive could spark them into further speculation about your well-being ("Hmmm, she's awfully emotional, could be an eating disorder!" People can be ignorant that way). You can, of course, mention how much fun both you and your fiancé are having at the boot camp you signed up for, or how much you're enjoying cooking healthier, how much more energy you have, and so on. Then move right on to another topic.

Now if you're dropping weight through extreme measures, and your friends are mentioning their concerns out of love for you, here's your script: "Thanks for your concern. I guess the workout regimen I undertook is a little too extreme, so I'm working with a trainer now to create a healthier plan. You know me, though. I always give things 100 percent." Right now, just thank these people for loving you enough, and having the courage, to express their concern.

**Q.** What's the best way to find out a guest's new partner's name?

**A.** Don't be afraid to be direct. Just call up the friend and use this wording:

"We're working on our guest list and we want to make sure we have the correct spelling of your [girlfriend's/partner's/husband's] name, as well as whether or not [he or she] has any titles, such as doctor or esquire, captain or lieutenant." Guests love it when you're so directly considerate.

This is far better than calling a parent to ask, as the parent might have outdated information. You so wouldn't want to send the invitation to your friend and his *last* partner. Ouch.

**Q.** I'm pregnant, and some of our guests are very old-world. How do I handle the questions they ask, like "don't you think it's wrong to get married in your condition?"

**A.** Some people cling to their beliefs, and if they ask the question, your best diplomacy is to step aside and let that veiled insult just fly right by you. Instead of getting into a debate about religion and premarital pregnancy, just use this script: "We've been so blessed, and we're happy to share our wedding with our entire family." You, my friend, have class.

**Q.** As we're planning the wedding, my friend is going through a divorce. How can I act normal and talk about my wedding without upsetting her?

**A.** It might seem like avoiding the topic of your wedding is the right course of action when this heartbroken friend is around, but that will only make her feel uncomfortable and remind her of her newly broken marital status. You're absolutely right to look for a way to act normal and talk about the wedding with her. Stick to the details—the food, the flowers, the gown, the fun stuff. And read her body language and reactions well. A divorcing person can have ups and downs, times when she's fine with talking about weddings and other times when any mention of a wedding reminds her of her own. Just honor this very necessary stage of her healing. If you sense she's clenching up, ask, "Would you like to talk about this another time?" and she may nod with relief at the chance to talk about *Lost* or *American Idol* or your planned girls' getaway to Portugal in the spring. The important thing is to keep treating her like the friend she's always been, and make sure you have an equal discussion going on. Listen as much as you talk, and if she needs to vent, be there for her.

**Q.** I've admittedly neglected my friends as I planned my wedding this year. I missed a lot of girls' nights out and friends' parties, and I'm nervous to invite these friends to the wedding now.

**A.** Don't invite them without working on the relationship first. Send each a great, handwritten note on a monogrammed or graphic-printed card—which is a class act and not a cop-out—with your friendly greeting and a good-natured apology. Your script is: "I am so sorry I've been all wrapped up in the wedding for so long, and that I've neglected you! I miss you and would love to get together with you for cof-

fee or lunch, or maybe we can plan a girls' night out sometime soon. Again, I'm sorry to have missed so much over the
past six months, and I can't wait to catch up with all that's
going on in your life. Love, [you]." It's that last part that's just
as important as the apology. You're being tremendously and
admirably diplomatic by showing interest in what's going on
in your friend's life, which will be very welcome by her. She'll
appreciate that you're showing that you value her news and
are interested in it, and not just planning to get together with
her to talk about your wedding.

Do this soon, since it would be a little too obvious if you
want to reconnect the week before the wedding so they will
come and give you gifts. At least, that is very likely to be their
assumption if you've been a no-show to all of their invitations. Your friends can smell opportunism, so be 100 percent
genuine in working on the relationships again, being yourself,
enjoying their company, and stepping out of wedding world
for a great night out.

**Q.** How do I handle friends who are upset
about not being in the bridal party? Act like nothing
happened?

**A.** No, avoidance isn't an effective diplomacy measure.
If any of your friends are upset about not being in the bridal
party, you can go to them with a simple and effective, "I'm
very sorry that you're disappointed"—and use the word "disappointed," not "angry" or "mad" or "hurt"—"that I couldn't

include you in the bridal party," and use the word "couldn't."
"But with all of [groom's] sisters, my sister, and my closest
friends since the first grade, it would have been a thirty-per-
son lineup if I could include all the people I wanted to. It was
disappointing for me, too, to have to draw the line. You're one
of my closest friends, and I'm quite sad that you're upset." No
need to start dropping names about who else you left out of
the bridal party. This is enough to express your own disappointment and reassure your friends that you do value their
friendship.

**Q.** Several gifts didn't arrive, and it's been months
since our wedding. How do we call to make sure our
guests' gifts weren't lost in the mail. We don't want
them to think we're just not thanking them.

**A.** The more directly you address this, the better. This is
one for a phone call or an in-person approach.

**YOU:** "We're getting our thank you notes list together,"
is a great way to open this chat, as it shows your gra-
ciousness in a way that "hey, your gift never showed
up" doesn't. "And we don't have any record of your gift
arriving." Now this only works if they said they sent
a gift. You can't make an assumption because guests
have up to a year after the wedding to send a gift. "I
thought I'd check with you to make sure your present
didn't get lost in the mail."

**YOUR GUEST:** "We ordered something off of your registry, and it was supposed to be sent to you." They may be embarrassed, so use your empathy here.

**YOU:** "I was nervous to call you about this, but I thought it would be best for you to know so that you can check with the registry. I'd hate for you to be charged for something that they never sent out." You're looking out for them as well. "And we didn't want you to think we just weren't sending a thank you." You're so gracious in the face of this very nerve-racking diplomacy issue. After all, you *are* calling to say "where's our gift?" but you aren't putting the emphasis on you. You're just taking care of business.

If the guest says that the gift is on order, your best response is:

**YOU:** "Great. We'll look forward to seeing it when it does arrive." Don't use the words "show up," which have a negative connotation. And don't get off the phone right away. Tell the guest it was great to see her at the wedding, and ask about what's going on in her life. Spend some time connecting so that it's not obvious you were just interested in her gift. Guests hate that.

Now if she sent a card and check that didn't get to you, she'll be very happy to hear from you, since she can track and cancel her check, not fear a theft. Wouldn't you want to know if a check you sent never arrived?

Have a light tone with this one, as it is one of those awkward topics that are best handled with a light diplomatic touch, a sense of humor, and an "I'm genuinely looking out for you" style.

**Q.** We need to postpone the wedding. How do we best handle this?

**A.** Make this job easier on yourselves by sending out printed announcements. Your best diplomacy comes through in the wording of an official statement, not a phone call to five people and a big game of telephone that kicks up the gossip mill about why you're postponing. It's all in the wording you use . . . an official, formal printed note of "[Your parents' names] announce the postponement of the wedding of [your names]" may follow traditional etiquette, but that one tends to set off some red flags. There's no explanation, and it does seem ominous to some guests. A better way to do this is to add some of your own "voice" to your announcement, something that provides an understandable reason, doesn't worry your guests, and offers diplomacy in full disclosure. Consider these possibilities:

*The countdown to our wedding has been reset!*
*Due to our plans to buy a house and our hectic schedules,*
*We've decided to postpone our wedding*

*Until the fall (which is our favorite time of year).*
*We'll be in touch shortly with the new details.*
Love,
[Your Names]

Or

*The wedding planning details got to us!*
*Rather than turn into Bridezilla and Groomzilla,*
*We've decided to push back our wedding date*
*So that we have more time to plan our wedding . . . and enjoy it!*
*We'll be in touch shortly with the new wedding date and place.*
Our love,
[Your Names]

I've started off with the "nothing's wrong" categories, in case you're worried that your need to push back the wedding will get people concerned or somehow be embarrassing to you or to your families. But if something is wrong—and you're not sure there will be a wedding at all—then go with the formal, printed announcement mentioned first in this section. If alarm bells go off with the recipients, you may get a ton of support from your friends and family that will help you make your decision.

**Q.** **We need to cancel the wedding. What do we say to keep our business private?**

**A.** A printed announcement is called for here as well, since word of mouth is perhaps the least effective and least diplomatic way to break the news to all of your loved ones. An elegant formal card can announce, "We've decided to call off our wedding. We thank you for all of your love and support. [Your Names]." You could get more creative if you wish, too. You may have seen on television the story of a woman who printed up cards that were almost identical to her engagement announcement cards, only they read, "Picked the wrong guy. Gave him the wrong finger. Thank you for your support." I don't know if anyone will ever come up with anything more perfect than that for situations where the bride finds herself mistreated or betrayed—luckily finding out before the big day—and making the wise and brave choice to cancel the wedding. As with the postponement notice, your cards will likely elicit supportive phone calls from friends and family, and in this instance know that among those who want to know the story behind the breakup are a large number of people who want to help you through it.

As a matter of diplomacy, resist the urge to trash-talk your ex with others. Take the high road, have your dignity, and look forward to a new future that will be better for you.

Of course, maybe the decision to call off your wedding isn't a matter of betrayal or mistreatment, no scandal . . . just a very heartfelt mutual decision that marriage isn't in either of your best interests. Couples who make this discovery before the wedding show tremendous courage and self-respect, and the best of them respect each other. Countless brides and grooms in the past have "gone through with it" when they knew it wasn't right, so if you're among those who feel that the wedding is a mistake for both of you, take great care of yourself, and make life easier for yourself by practicing good diplomacy in how you answer others' questions.

Just say: "We both decided this was just not a good move for us. We're wonderful friends, but we both take marriage very seriously. It just wasn't right for us."

**Q.** Since we're canceling the wedding, we need to return the gifts we've received. I didn't save the gift receipts for them to get their money back, so how do I handle this?

**A.** There are way too many couples out there who "forget" to return their gifts. As a matter of class, you return everything that was given to you in preparation for your married life together. And when you lose the gift receipts, you approach each guest personally, with a phone call, to let them know you're in a bind. Here is your script:

"I'm returning your gift with my thanks, but I'm sorry to say that I didn't keep the gift receipts for any of the gifts to be returned. So I'm very sorry for the inconvenience, and I do hope you'll be able to return it with your purchase receipts for the sale. I know that the online registry has a record of you buying it, and their customer support number is. . . ."

Try to help in any way you can, never leaving the legwork to them. Provide that customer service number or a link to the frequently asked questions section on the registry page that gives return instructions.

Guests love honesty, and they love knowing that you have their interests at heart. Thank them again for their generosity, and be sure to ship the item back to them via tracked postal service, wrapped ultra-securely to protect the item. When you show care for the gift, you show care for the giver.

**Q.** We had a death in the family one month before our wedding, and our relatives—even ones who are not invited to the wedding!—think it would be too soon for us to have our wedding. We'd like to go ahead with our plans, as we think it's what our deceased relative would have wanted.

**A.** There's undoubtedly been a lot of discussion among your wedding guests as to whether or not your wedding will still take place. Your crowd is no doubt divided as to the propriety of holding a wedding, since they're all in varying stages of grief depending on how close they each were to the departed. "He would have wanted the wedding to take place" is the mantra of some, while others can't imagine dressing up and dancing when something so tragic has taken place. Whatever their position, they're waiting to hear a definitive word from you.

Good diplomacy doesn't do well in the grapevine or telephone game, with word passed from person to person and altered ever so slightly with each conversation, so your best bet is to send out a printed announcement to the relatives who have been affected by the situation.

*With honor to Grandma's belief that the family should be together,*
*And that love should be celebrated,*
*We have decided that our wedding will go on as planned.*
*We look forward to seeing you at our celebration.*
Love,
[Your Names]

Or

*With great thought and consideration to our family and friends,*
*As well as to what Grandma would surely have wanted,*
*We have decided to go forward with our wedding plans.*
*We know that Grandma will be there with us all in spirit,*
*Smiling as she watches her grandchildren at play*
*And her beloved family celebrating one of life's greatest joys.*
Our love,
[Your Names]

The key is your tone. The above samples show a great reverence for what Grandma would have loved about the continuation of the wedding plans, and they stay positive. They don't make mention of the family's grief, as in "We know you are all still hurting from the loss of [loved one], but we have decided to go on with our wedding plans." There's a slippery little tone of selfishness in that particular note, a subtle "we know you're hurting, but we decided you've grieved long enough." Stay far away from any declaration that the grieving is now over because you're the center of the action now, and don't defend yourselves by saying the wedding was planned before Grandma got sick. You're writing to people who may still be raw from the loss, and the diplomatic notes here show your respect for Grandma's wishes.

Some couples take this loss and turn it into something good. On this note, they mention Grandma's cherished cause, asking guests to honor Grandma's memory by supporting her favorite charity. You might provide the Web site for the Leukemia and Lymphoma Society, or for the animal shelter for which she volunteered. Some brides and grooms ask their guests to bring canned food and nonperishable goods to the wedding for a massive donation to the food pantry or shelter Grandma supported. This gesture pays homage to her, and guests love being able to perform an act that honors Grandma's goodness. Your wedding, then, is not 100 percent about you. You've included Grandma by adding an element of benevolence that is so her.

As for those who blow up with a "how could you be so selfish?" note or phone call, just understand that people handle their grief differently, especially if there's an element of tragedy or unfairness about the departed person's death. Listen to them with empathy, and tell them, "We're grieving too. We

spent a lot of time thinking about this, and we know without a doubt that Grandma would not have wanted any special
family gathering to be canceled." Not "our wedding"—say
"any special family gathering" instead. The words "our wedding" can be loaded with assumptions on the listener's end. I,
me, mine, ours . . . leave these words out as best you can.

Guests are, of course, free to revoke their positive RSVP if
they're not ready to celebrate at your wedding, so your best
diplomacy is to accept their decision, not fight them on it.
People do what they have to do. Just send them a gracious
note with no semblance of judgment in it. "Dear [relatives'
names]: Thank you for your note. We completely understand
your decision, as we know how close you were to Grandma.
Please do call us for a dinner get-together sometime soon, as
we'd love to spend time with you. All our love, [your names]."
Your fine diplomacy let them off the hook, and expressed a
wish to get together in the future.

Make sure the notes you send out contain a new RSVP at
the bottom of the card, with a message: "Please let us know if
you will be unable to attend. Regrets only, by [date] at [your
phone number] or at [your e-mail address]. Thank you." The
simple fact that you offer this option shows your sensitivity to
your guests' belief systems.

**Q.** **We want to create a honeymoon registry, but
wouldn't it be rude to ask our guests to pay for our
getaway?**

**A.** No, not at all. No diplomacy needed here either, provided you offer this registry as one of several choices. Create a traditional registry and a honeymoon registry, so that your guests can decide on their own what they'd most like to get you. You're not telling them what to buy, and you're not offering this fairly new option as their only choice. Guests love taking part in this, and they won't be offended at your offering it. Those guests who are more traditional can look for the blender on your traditional home registry.

**Q.** We're being pressured to plan a post-wedding celebration after our destination wedding. People who aren't invited to our very small wedding in Hawaii keep asking when we're going to have a party they can attend.

**A.** While some couples make the decision to host a big gathering for all of their extended family and friends after they return from a destination wedding, you can explain that you're not following that trend: "We have no plans for a post-wedding celebration right now, but if we do decide to plan one, we'll definitely let you know." That's it. You don't need to talk about how you're putting your wedding gift money toward a house, or how your small budget led you to plan a destination wedding in the first place. Explanations are not needed, even if people tell you "that's how it's done" with destination weddings. You've handled the rude, fishing-for-an-invitation question with brilliant diplomacy.

# Chapter 7

# Child's Play:
# Handling the Kids

This is always a tough one. Guests want to bring their kids to the wedding for many reasons. First of all, they may have to travel to attend your wedding and don't wish to leave their kids with relatives at home, or with babysitters at your wedding site. That's a pretty strong argument, as any parent would be nervous about leaving their little ones with babysitters they don't know. Second, they might live far away from all of the family and friends, and your wedding is a chance for everyone to meet their kids, perhaps for the first time. Ours is a global society, and many people have moved clear across the country for work or to live in a different region with a different feel. A wedding these days is more like a family reunion in that sense, so they're imagining a terrific reception where their kids can be adorably dressed up and interacting with their cousins. Understandable, but as you'll see in this chapter, you have diplomatic solutions to both of these scenarios.

Leaving kids off of a wedding guest list is often a couple's tough-but-necessary decision. Given their budget limits, and perhaps a space issue when that perfect site they found only holds 150 people—it's just not possible to allow guests to bring kids. Especially in families where there are a lot of kids, or if you have a circle of friends who are all having their babies and building their families now.

And of course, there's a style element that makes many couples leave kids off the guest list. They want a formal, elegant wedding where their guests mingle with flutes of champagne in their hands and the menu is gourmet and delectable. Oysters, not Oreos. Syrah, not sippy cups.

The issue of kids at a wedding opens up a creaky door of complications. If you're allowing your sister and brother to bring their kids, and others find out, wanting equal treatment with a suspiciously juvenile whine of "Why them and not us?" If the kids who are invited are known to be holy terrors or bratty biters, you're in the unenviable position of telling parents whose egos are all wrapped up in the scenario that their little cherubs didn't make the cut. That's where the trouble begins—when the parents make it all about themselves. How do you handle that?

Diplomacy is essential when it comes to problems with kids, perhaps more than with any other group on your list due to the deep feelings of the parents. These are kids we're talking about. Parents love them and want to protect them, to share them, and the love of a parent can sometimes cloud other realities. It's very important to remember that, so that you don't fuel a conflict that is tiny, or create one that isn't there at all.

**Q.** I've heard that several guests are going to bring their kids to the wedding, even though we said not to. Should we fight it or just plan a kids' table?

**A.** If you said "No kids, please" to all of your guests—whether through the wording of your invitations ("Mr. and Mrs. John Smith" written on the invitation without "and Family" means no kids invited) or through a very direct communication such as an insert in your invitation with details on babysitting plans and contacts—you must stick to your decision. Giving in, being passive, and setting up a kids' table for those who broke the rules—or rather, disrespected your request—sets you up for a huge diplomacy problem at the wedding. Imagine: 95 percent of other guests made arrangements for childcare, left the kids with their parents, or hired a babysitter, and then they walk in to your wedding to see a dozen kids running around. Eyebrows will furrow, and those who followed your request may get annoyed, angry, or resentful . . . perhaps at you. "Why are they rewarding the people who brought their kids?" and "Hey, we paid for a babysitter!" and "My parents canceled their weekend plans to watch our kids!" heats up the anger factor pretty quickly, which is not the mood you want at your wedding. Rampant kids, angry guests, you looking like a wimp—these are not the aftereffects of good diplomacy.

They're going to come at you one of two ways. Indirectly, a parent could pass along a message to . . . oh . . . your mother, who she knows would have a better chance of swaying you into allowing just this one teeny-weeny, little exception. That's very shrewd, because your mother might play "the good guy" in their conversation and assure the pushy parent that she'll get you to say okay. The indirect approach is multi-pronged, creating a few different branches of diplomatic uh-ohs for you: the request and facing your mother, or your message-bearing relative.

When Mom or any other message-bearer puts a hand on your arm, looks at you with that blinky-eyelashes expression and perhaps unconsciously goes for those guilt strings with a "Your cousin really doesn't want to leave the kids with a sitter, since they're just babies, so can't you just make an exception for her?" remember that your cousin has many, many options at her disposal. Yes, it would be convenient for her to bring the twins to the wedding, but she has left the building without her kids before. She does have resources. Her parents are nearby. Your response to your mother cuts out her middleman power:

> **YOU:** "How about this? I'll give [cousin] a call to help her figure out a plan for the kids' care. A lot of people are bringing their own sitters along for the trip so that they have caretakers they trust for their kids, the kids

are comfortable with a sitter they know, and the parents can just relax and enjoy a few hours on their own."

**MOM:** "But I already told her it would be okay!"

Keep your cool. This is an age-old method. Mom is depending on you to be afraid of (1) confrontation, (2) letting someone down, and (3) going against what Mom said.

**YOU:** "I know you were just trying to help out because you're so thoughtful, but there's plenty of time for me to help her figure out a babysitting plan for the kids. I know you already told her that she could bring the twins, but I'm quite sad about being in the position of having to limit the guest list, so I have to do what I have to do to make it as easy as I can on all of the guests with kids. We already told everyone that we couldn't allow kids at the reception, and [fiancé] and I already agreed that we won't make any exceptions for anyone, because we don't want to hurt anyone's feelings."

Now go for Mom's protection: "We wouldn't want any-one to be mad at you for making an exception for [cousin], so we have to be firm about our decision because it's fair to absolutely everyone. You won't be in the hot seat, we won't be in the hot seat, and no one will be angry at [cousin] at the wedding." Mom wouldn't want any of *that*. "So don't worry about already telling her that she can bring the kids. How about this? I'll be more than happy to tell her that I wasn't clear enough with you about our no-kids rule, and that while you had her best interests at heart, we just have to say no. Sadly, it's a no. And then I'll help her come up with a plan for childcare during the wedding, or tell her about what everyone else is doing with their kids. Our other cousin is letting her kids stay with friends' families for a weekend sleepover, which the kids are excited about. One of our friends is bringing her regular babysitter along on a free vacation weekend—her babysitter from home watches the kids during the wedding and reception, and then she's free to spend the afternoons on her own. They're giving her $100 spending money. So I have plenty of ideas to help out."

You just beautifully defused one of the most complicated diplomacy issues regarding parents pushing kids onto the guest list. When you call your cousin with a friendly demeanor, empathizing with her situation ("My mom mentioned that you were wondering about bringing the kids to the wedding" is diplomacy gold, rather than "My mom said you're bringing the kids to the wedding." Subtle wording, but very effective), you eliminate the maneuvering and get right to the part where you work with her to create a solution. One that doesn't involve the twins coming to the wedding.

The key to this conversation is that your cousin tried to avoid talking directly to you, but now you're on the phone with her, gracious and kind, willing to share a list of

possibilities that you've already arranged. That's quite generous of you.

Try saying: "[Cousin], we have so many guests who are in
your same situation that we've been telling everyone the following suggestions. . . ."

Use the word "suggestions." It's way better than saying,
"This is how you need to do it." No one likes to be told what
to do with their kids

Now, for the parents who go directly to you with their
request that you let them bring the kids: If you are blindsided
by an unexpected phone call, tell the person that you'll get
back to them. As any diplomacy expert knows, it's often an
extended period of time between the asking of the question
and delivering the answer that gives you an advantage.

Now let's say that the parent calls and asks you directly when
you're not rushed, hurried, busy, or distracted. That shows a
large amount of consideration on their part, and maturity and
good communication skills on their part as well. Thank them
for coming to you directly (without slamming those who
didn't—very important), and then explain that you wish you
could allow guests to bring kids, but there's just not enough
space, or budget, and it opens a huge can of worms for you if
you make any exceptions.

**YOU:** "It's very difficult for us to have to uphold this
rule, since we love all the kids. And that's why we
planned a babysitter room for during the reception, as
well as some group events for the wedding weekend."

**PUSHY PARENT:** "But the kids can sit with us!" Understand that some parents aren't comfortable being away from small children, so apply your best empathy.

**YOU:** "The kiddie room will be literally next door (or in a hotel room upstairs) so all of the parents will be stopping in to check on the kids during the wedding."

What if you haven't made babysitting plans or didn't book a kiddie room next to the wedding? Your response would be, "I'm very sorry, but we really have to stick with our no-kids rule."

When you stand up for your decision, and prevent any guests from wedging their kids into your guest list, you'll have a tremendous amount of respect for yourself. When you're strong with the first few, your diplomacy spreads.

**Q.** We have received several response cards where guests wrote in that they were bringing their kids. They didn't ask, they just told us that they're bringing the kids though the response card.

**A.** These guests are hoping that you won't have a spine, that you're so exhausted at this point from planning your wedding that you won't say anything in response to them, and they can save on babysitter's fees. The best diplomatic approach is to call them directly—no e-mail, no voice mail. Let them know first that you're so happy that they, the adults, will be attending your wedding, but. . . .

Say to them: "I noticed that you added the kids to the response card, and I'm very sorry but we've had to make the decision that this is an adults-only reception. A few people wrote in that their kids would attend, and we're calling them all right now."

You've just given them the equal treatment message—that you're not singling them out or leaving out their kids—and you're letting them hear in your voice that you're sticking to your guns with kindness and understanding toward them. You'll then let them know about the alternative childcare plans that you have. But it's your directly contacting them with your firm stand that makes this wise diplomacy. It might be the case that they weren't being sneaky at all, that they simply don't know the etiquette rule that when an invitation is addressed only to Mr. and Mrs. John Smith, the kids aren't invited.

## Keeping the Peace

The direct contact approach is absolutely essential. Good diplomacy is about clear communication, and your voice is a conductor of that. An e-mail can be taken as a slap with its flat message and no voice inflection. Make the call.

And after you take care of the business at hand, make sure you ask them how things are with them, ask how the kids are enjoying school, how their vacation was, and so on. Just a bit of small talk takes the sting out of being turned down for their request to bring their kids, and shows you as the gracious person you are.

**Q.** What do we do if guests just show up with kids at the wedding?

**A.** Every now and then, guests disregard your instructions, or they just didn't understand the way a wedding invitation and response card works. Some lose their childcare at the last second, and it's either they bring the children or they don't show up for your wedding at all. Whatever the reason, good or bad, it's your diplomatic move in the moment. Resist the urge to get angry, and look for the solution. If you already have childcare set up for those guests who requested it, you'll just need to let the guests know where to drop off their kids. Your greeting, or your parents' pre-planned greeting when they see guests arrive with the kids, would be: "Hello! We're so glad you could make it to the wedding. The babysitter is upstairs with the kids, in room 499, and we have movies and pizza for them up there. [Friend's name] will take you up there." Appoint a friend to be your go-to person, who runs these little errands when situations come up at the ceremony or the reception. Usually, your happy demeanor and direct instructions are enough to take care of the problem. No need to lecture or scold, since you don't know yet why they just brought their kids along to the wedding. The temptation is to jump to a negative conclusion, but you never know what's actually going on. So be gracious, guide them to the solution, and move on.

What happens if you don't have childcare set up at the site? Well, you can't tell the guests to turn around and take the kids home, so go to the site manager with the situation. He or she is well-schooled in these mini-party-crasher situations, with an expert ability to have the staff do some quick place-setting at the parents' table for kids' seating. I've seen site staff members put together a smaller kids' table in minutes. The site manager will no doubt assure you that this little fire is easily put out, and that you should put it out of your mind. Let the expert handle the technicalities, and you'll handle the business end later. Your diplomacy is often just handing off the challenge to the expert and not getting angry, not stewing or fuming, not avenging the etiquette slight with a barbed comment or a guilt trip. Sometimes you can't do anything about the things that go wrong at a wedding, but what you *can* do is handle them with grace and keep your mind on the higher purpose of the day.

**Q.** If guests do bring kids to the wedding uninvited, and we do have the site manager set up the table for them, how do we handle all the guests who see this and get angry?

**A.** Very understandable. And you will see many guests raising an eyebrow and wondering why they didn't get the same option. Some of the less mannered will come up to you for an explanation, which you don't owe them. But here's your best diplomatic answer: "[Parents] lost their babysitter at the last minute, so it was either this or we wouldn't have had them at our wedding at all. I'm sure it upset them to get the last-second cancellation from their sitter, so we're all just doing the best we can." No complaining about how they should have called four hours ago. No conspiring with the offended guest about how rude some people can be in an effort to make this guest feel better. That kind of thing gets around. Just remind the guest of your higher perspective: "We're just glad that they are here with us today."

## Keeping the Peace

Share this advice with your parents, as many guests will go to them with this particular complaint. Great wedding diplomacy extends to your parents, whether or not they're official hosts of the wedding.

**Q.** How can we make sure guests take their crying babies out of our ceremony space? They haven't at other weddings.

**A.** Don't you hate that? Parents don't want to miss out on seeing the ceremony, or be inconvenienced by walking outside with their kids, so they just let their little ones scream. Or, even worse, their little cherub sees your wedding as a great opportunity to get attention, so he calls out with comments or jokes, or just makes sounds . . . loudly. Some guests might laugh at how precocious he is, and that just encourages him to continue. You can't just turn around while in the middle of taking your vows and scream "Get your brat out of here!"—as much as you might want to—so the solution is a preemptive diplomacy effort. Here are your options:

1. Let someone outside of the bridal party and your parents know that you're concerned about the kids, who have been known to cause major distractions at other weddings. Your script would be: "If the kids act up, would you please walk over to [child's parent] and ask her to take the kids out to the vestibule? Tell her you're concerned that we won't be able to hear our vows on the videotape." Very often, a parent with truly disruptive kids will have heard this request before, but even if they haven't, it can be quite motivating when someone is standing right there in front of them, asking them to take it outside. If that doesn't work, if the parent manages to shush the children—for now—as clever little kids are wise enough to do when they see another adult that they don't have wrapped around their finger making a complaint, and thus fearing punishment—here is option two:

2. Prearrange for the officiant to instruct about the rules at the start of the ceremony: "While we adore and appreciate the rambunctiousness of youth, we hope that you will take your children outside to the garden sanctuary if they can't sit quietly. Thank you." Delivered with a smile,

and from the authority figure, this instruction usually does the trick.

3. You can also print it in your wedding program that the children are loved, but you request that parents will take their kids outside to the garden if the long ceremony proves to be too much for the kids.

4. And you can also prearrange for kids to be entertained in a side room at the ceremony. The parents might enjoy your ceremony much more, knowing that their kids are well monitored and having fun in another area. Remember, most parents don't enjoy being the target of raised eyebrows and quiet judgment of their parenting skills. What some people see as parental indifference when kids act up could be just the parent freezing and hoping for the moment to pass.

**Q.** I'm worried that my five year-old nephew is going to misbehave during the ceremony. We made him a ring bearer because we didn't want to leave him out.

**A.** Most couples worry about how the little ones are going to behave. Your good diplomacy here is in preempting as much as you can, with two eye-to-eye meetings with the child and his parents—one conversation a month before the wedding and then another the night before. Again, most kids respond pretty well to authority figures who are not their parents, when mixed with the authority of their parents. This meeting is your own little diplomacy summit. You must start off your "talks" as if you're positive he has it within him to behave.

Say to him: "[Child's name], we wanted to talk with you and your parents about what you'll need to do during our wedding. As the ring bearer, you have a very important job to do that we know you'll be great at" is a good way to start. Explain what he'll be doing, how easy it is, and that it's only going to take fifteen minutes (if you'll have a short ceremony), or that he'll just have to hand the ring to the best man and then go sit with his parents.

Sometimes kids act out because they're unsure in a social situation, so if he knows he's only on a fifteen minute act-your-best schedule, he has parameters he can understand. Let him know as much as possible about the scenario:

"You'll be walking down the aisle by yourself. Is that okay with you?" gives the child a little bit of control over what he can and can't handle. A five year-old might want to walk down the aisle with his parents. He may not want to walk down the aisle holding hands with his big sister, the flower girl. That right there is what sets off so many other ring bearers—they're forced to "look adorable" and some kids are too willful to be posed. As one ring bearer put it, "I am not a puppy!" Your diplomacy talks with the ring bearer and his parents will reveal his sensitivities, so that you won't court disaster by treating him like . . . oh . . . a trained puppy.

And then there's the reward. Yes, it's bribery, but it works.

Try saying: "[Child's name], if you act like a good little man and walk down the aisle, stand next to [adult], walk forward with the rings, listen during the ceremony, then walk back down the aisle and pose for pictures afterward, we're going to get you the new PlayStation game you wanted. If you don't behave yourself, you don't get your prize." Kids love prizes, and positive reinforcement for a job well done. Considering how important your ceremony is, it's likely you'll find that a generous gift to the child attendant is worth the investment.

Just talk to the parents first before you make a prize offer. They may not want their child to have a video game. Keep a sense of humor when you're talking with the child, and with the parents. If you're too serious and try to tell them how good parents would have a well-mannered child, that's anti-diplomacy. Never put them on the defensive, and keep your statements to the event at hand. Never mention the child's previous outbursts, like "Considering that your son ruined our cousin's wedding by singing a Wiggles song throughout the entire ceremony, we thought we'd set some ground rules." Don't dip into the past to try to influence good behavior in the future. Thank the parents for all they'll be doing in preparation for the wedding, as they always appreciate a little positive reinforcement too.

**Q.** We told our junior bridesmaids' parents to choose appropriate dresses for them, and now they say they bought black strapless dresses for them. They're twelve, and it's inappropriate. I'd like them to choose different dresses.

**A.**   You have every right in the world to request more appropriate dresses for the twelve-year-olds. Since part of diplomacy is admitting your part in any dilemma—it would have been better if you had asked the parents to check their choice with you before buying them—admit that graciously.

Say to them: "I regret that I didn't have time to go with you to the store, since this change could have been avoided." Not, "Well, I wish you had checked with me first!" The first is solution-focused, the second is blaming. Blaming never gets you where you want to go. So explain to the parents that you must request a change of attire for the girls. You'll need to work together to get the dresses returned and find more appropriate choices.

**PARENTS:** "What's wrong with the dresses?"

**YOU:** "The sexy style would just look wrong when stood next to the more classic and less revealing style of the older bridesmaids. Now, let's find a way to make them work. I know of a great kids' accessory store where we can get the girls inexpensive jackets that will look gorgeous on them and coordinate well with the bridesmaids' dress styles. They're only $20 each, and this will keep you from having to buy new dresses."

You presented your reason without over-explaining, delivered the solution, and showed your concern for the parents' budget.

**Q.** One of our flower girls said she doesn't want to be in the bridal party. She's afraid to walk down the aisle in front of all those people. Her parents are telling her not to be a quitter.

**A.** This is a tough, tough position to be in. Visit with the parents and the child if you can—if not, a phone call will do—and find out what would make the child most comfortable.

**YOU:** "Would you feel better about walking down the aisle side-by-side with one of the bridesmaids?" That's a common solution that many kids like.

**FLOWER GIRL:** "No. . . ."

**YOU:** "What don't you like about the idea of walking down the aisle with all those people around?" Don't use the words "what are you afraid of?" or "what makes you nervous?" since those very words can set back your diplomacy work.

**FLOWER GIRL:** "I'm afraid of tripping, since the dress is so long." There's your answer. Hem up the dress a bit more. Diplomacy often uncovers a different problem underneath, one you didn't suspect.

If the child insists that she doesn't want to be in the bridal party, she isn't to be pushed. You really don't want a sullen, angry, or terrified flower girl—right? Everyone in your bridal party should want to be there.

**YOU:** "Okay, you don't have to walk down the aisle. But would you still like to be my flower girl at the wedding?"

**FLOWER GIRL:** "I can?"

**YOU:** "Yes. You can sit with your parents, or if you'd like, you can be our greeter, handing out the wedding programs or the wedding bubble bottles, together with your other cousins." Many kids like the safety in numbers, they can avoid the super-serious tone of the ceremony spotlight, and they still get an important job for the wedding.

If the parents seem disappointed in their daughter, handle this diplomacy side-effect with humor.

"Oh, I didn't like being in bridal parties when I was her age, so I can completely understand her wishes." Yes, use the word "wishes," not "fears" or "concerns." "I just want her to be happy and comfortable on the wedding day, and she'll still be listed as flower girl in the program, and she'll be in the pictures. I'm quite pleased with this agreement, since she's such a friendly girl. She'll do great at the wedding."

Their daughter just learned a very important lesson, actually—it is okay to speak up when you're being asked to do something you're uncomfortable with.

**Q.** I'm getting pressure to include my cousin's kids as flower girls, and my cousin already told the girls they'd be chosen.

**A.** When word gets to you about a promise that's been made in your name to two innocent children, call the cousin directly to explain your distress that a miscommunication has happened. Not "You're manipulating me!" or "You're a control freak"—both of which may be true—but use wording that glosses over the slight.

Don't bother trying to find out the reasons or who may have told her it was okay (your mother might be shaking in her espadrilles right now if she gave a green light). Your diplomatic goal is to remove the children from the bridal party, correct (not condemn) the cousin even if she deserves it, and take this one off your plate.

> **YOU:** "[Cousin], I just heard that your girls are under the impression that they're my flower girls?" Use "are under the impression"—not "were told by you."

> She will see what's coming.

> **COUSIN:** "The girls are thrilled. They've never been flower girls before."

**YOU:** "Well, I wish they could be, but we've only chosen my sister's girls to be the flower girls. I've had to turn down quite a few others, and that was not a pleasant decision to make, since I know how much little girls want to be in a bridal party. So I do need you to tell them there's been a mistake, that they won't be flower girls, but I would like them to be special wedding party attendants at the ceremony. Their cousins are going to be handing out the programs and bubble bottles, and that would be a perfect way for your girls to do something special on the big day. Or, they can be my favor assistants, handing out favors to guests at the reception. Which do you think they'd like to do?"

Brava! You eliminated the problem and gave the mother alternative options. In special circumstances like these, where kids have gotten their hopes up, you absolutely must have some sort of special offering for them. It's not their fault that their mother had bad etiquette (and some nerve!), so they shouldn't be on the receiving end of what can feel to a child like a social snub.

## Keeping the Peace

Good diplomacy sometimes hinges on what you don't say.

If the mother is truly a weasel and says that you should tell her kids, turn down her order with a laugh and a simple, "No, I think this news should come from you." No need to follow-up with "you're the one who told them they could be flower girls." That much is understood, and going there could be inflammatory.

Instead, say, "Please tell the girls I'm excited to have them as honor attendants at the wedding, along with their cousins," is a very nice sign-off to the conversation. You're restating that you've just created a positive solution, and the task of approaching the girls with the news stays right where it belongs—with the mother who overstepped her bounds.

If the pressure is coming from the mother, without the girls being told they will be flower girls, your response follows the same script as above, with or without the offer to be special program or favor presenters.

## Keeping the Peace

If you have a plan to keep the kids occupied, you won't need to depend on parents to keep the kids under control at what could be a non-kid-friendly event. Preplanning could prevent the need for any diplomacy.

**Q.** At other weddings, the kids ran wild. How can we get the parents to watch them during the reception?

**A.** This is one time that you don't need a middleman or the site's staff to smoothly create a solution. If the kids are running wild, you should approach the parents with a smile and direct their attention to where their kids are flinging oysters at the other guests.

"Can you please corral the kids before someone gets hurt?" is all that's needed. No big lecture, just the authority of your presence and a direct request for the parents to gather up their kids and perhaps make them sit at the table.

It gets tricky when the kids aren't being vandals, but are running around the room. In this case, it might be you who has to lighten up a little bit. Kids will be kids, and while children running full-speed through the reception wasn't a part of your original wedding dream, just take a look around at how much the guests are enjoying watching the little ones at play. You can, and should, tell the kids to take it easy and be careful so that no one gets hurt, and that running through the table area is not allowed.

Be sure to stock the kids' table with plenty of games, coloring books, crafts, and kids' snacks to hold their attention.

# A Note from the Author

You can handle ANYTHING that people throw your way. Weddings do make people crazy, and you're often just in the wrong place at the wrong time, the recipient of someone else's issues.

It's my wish and hope that you've found relief and comfort
in many of the situations described in this book,
that they've been helping you with existing people problems,
and that you're keeping these insights in mind for future problems.
It's an honor for me to partner with you through these pages,
to help return your focus to the real joy of planning your wedding,
to the gift that is your relationship with your future husband.
It's all about your relationships—with him, and with all of your loved ones.
Please do send me your stories of how you conquered a diplomacy problem,
and we may add your story to future editions of this book.
Visit me, and submit your story, at www.sharonnaylor.net.

With love,
Sharon Naylor

# Index

# Index

not showing up, 190–92
from office, 193–95
paying for travel/lodging expenses,
  180
requesting special meals, 189–90
requesting spotlight dances, 197–99
seating arrangements, 199
uninviting, 200–201
your ex-boyfriend, 134–35

In-laws
feuding between, 5–8, 40–41
fiancé not supporting you vs.,
  116–24
fiancé sister as bridesmaid, 60–61
making disparaging remarks,
  34–35, 37–39
not liking you, 32–34
Invitations, 29, 45
declining recommended provider
  of, 201–2
divorced parents on, 46
relatives shirking responsibility of
  making, 186–88
save the dates and, 177, 181–82

Kids, 217–39
crying babies, 228–30
excluding from wedding, 219–24
general diplomacy tips, 217–19
getting parents to watch, 238–39
guest bringing without invitation,
  224–28
in wedding party, 230–38

Location, parents imposing will about,
  15–20

Parents, 1–56. See also Divorced parents;
  In-laws
accepting fiancé family help and,
  11–15

bragging about wedding details,
  27–28
breaking financial commitments,
  35–37
bringing controversial guests,
  25–27
changing wedding plans, 8–11
controlling planning and, 3–15,
  40–41, 116–24, 162–64,
  166–68
destination wedding complication
  with, 39–40
directing where guests stay, 41–42
general diplomacy tips, 1–2
his/hers, feuding over wedding
  plans, 5–8, 40–41
inviting people without
  authorization, 200–201
making disparaging remarks, 34–35
mother overspending on herself,
  43–45
obsessed with plans, 42–43
outdated etiquette of, 28–29
paying for wedding and, 3–5, 11–
  15, 22–23, 43–45, 50–52
refusing to toast at wedding, 48–49
religious demands from, 15–20
step-parent issues, 29–30, 31–32
thinking marriage is premature,
  20–22
threatening not to attend wedding,
  15–20
tributes to dead parents, 31–32
two-dad "giving away" dilemma,
  29–30
what they wear, 52–56
Partying, of wedding party, controlling,
  89–90, 98–101
Paying for wedding
accepting fiancé' family help, 11–15
asking parents for more money,
  50–52

245